"Thirty years in the making, *Rodney Scott's World of BBQ* takes its readers into the heart, mind, and soul of a barbecue artisan who is at the top of his craft. Rodney Scott 'goes whole hog' by accessibly and expertly guiding you through his barbecuing method. His recipes for side dishes, desserts, and beverages definitely remind you that, yes, every day will be a good day when you use this cookbook."

—ADRIAN MILLER, CULINARY HISTORIAN AND JAMES BEARD AWARD WINNER

"I love Rodney's classic and straightforward approach to BBQ . . . He is a true master of the pits. Watching him smoke a whole hog is an inspiration."

—MICHAEL SYMON, CHEF AND AUTHOR

"It's rare that someone who is such a master at what they do stands out equally for who they are. Rodney Scott tops both of those lists. In *Rodney Scott's World of BBQ* he shares his inspiring journey of passion and perseverance—fueled by the power of fellowship and damned fine food cooked from the heart and soul. Now you can cook alongside Rodney and make it a great day for those lucky enough to join you by your pit and at your table."

—DANNY MEYER, RESTAURATEUR AND AUTHOR OF SETTING THE TABLE: THE TRANSFORMING POWER OF HOSPITALITY IN BUSINESS

RODNEY SCOTT GREW UP WITH BARBECUE IN HIS BLOOD. He cooked his first whole hog when he was just eleven years old at his family's barbecue spot in Hemingway, South Carolina. Now, four decades later, he owns one of the country's most awarded and talked about barbecue destinations: Rodney Scott's BBQ. Coauthored with lauded writer Lolis Eric Elie and beautifully shot on location by Jerrelle Guy, Rodney's uplifting life story speaks to how hope, hard work, and a whole lot of optimism—along with recipes for the smokiest, most succulent pulled pork, ribs and barbecued chicken—helped to create a budding empire built on good will and good eating.

RODNEY SCOTT'S
WORLD OF BBQ

Every Day Is a Good Day

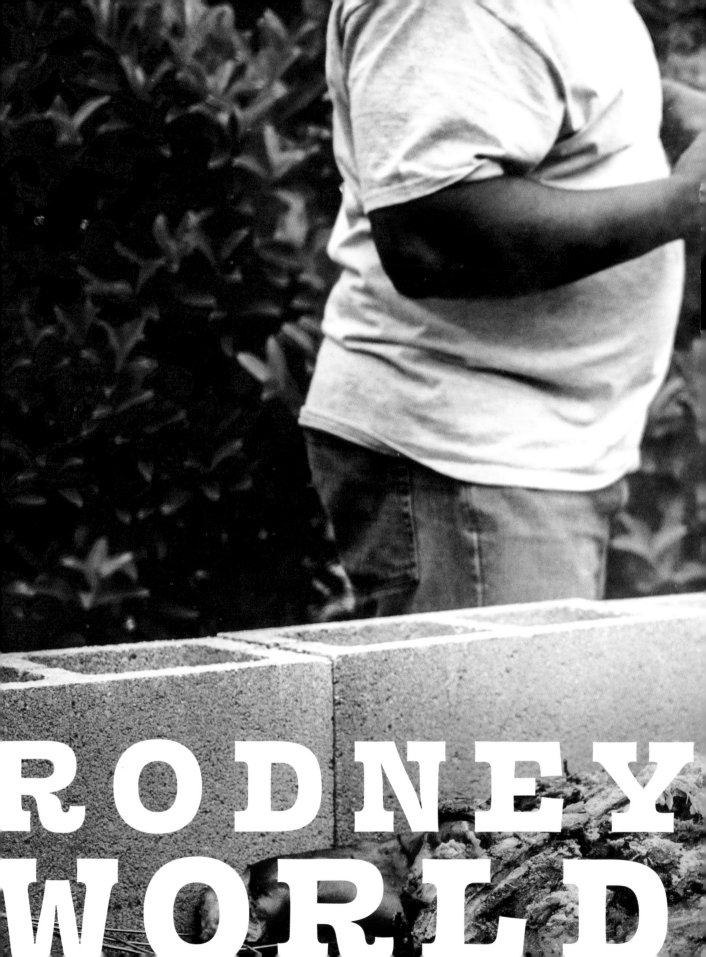

RODNEY
WORLD

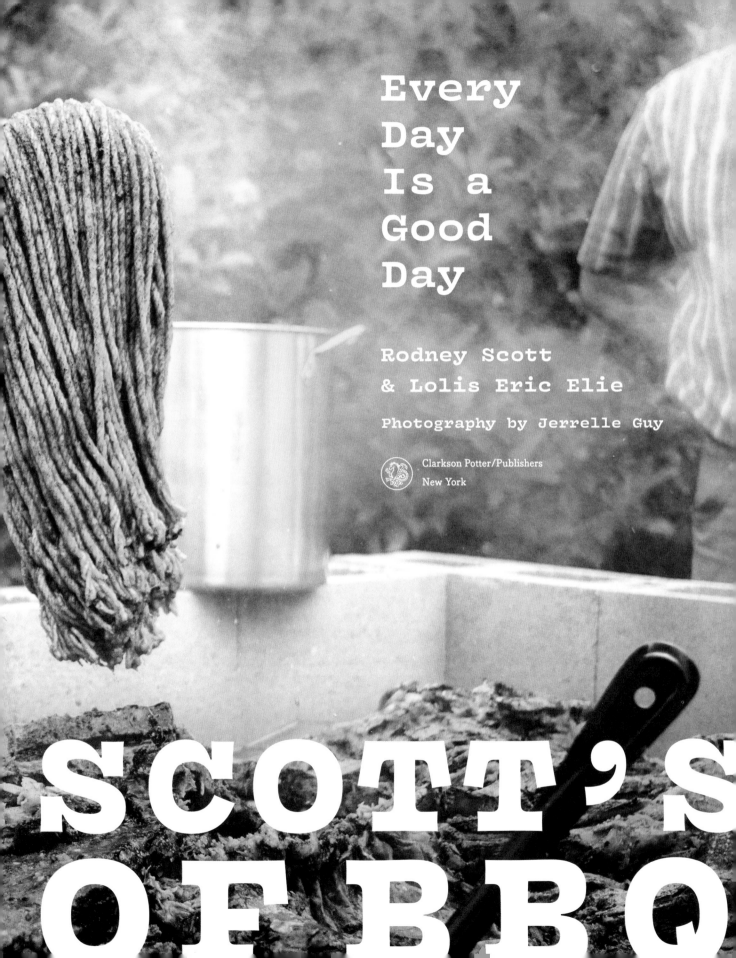

Every Day Is a Good Day

Rodney Scott
& Lolis Eric Elie

Photography by Jerrelle Guy

Clarkson Potter/Publishers
New York

SCOTT'S
OF BBQ

Library of Congress Control Number: 2020946687

ISBN 978-1-984-82693-0
Ebook ISBN 978-1-984-82694-7

Printed in Canada

Photographer: Jerrelle Guy
Assistant photographer: Eric Harrison
Editor: Raquel Pelzel
Designer: Jen Wang
Production editor: Mark McCauslin
Production manager: Kelli Tokos
Composition: Merri Ann Morrell
Indexer: Elizabeth T. Parson

10 9 8 7 6 5 4 3

First Edition

You won't see the name Suzanne Pihakis on many of these pages, but in a sense that name is written in invisible ink on every one. She's the backbone of the Pihakis Restaurant Group, and when Rodney Scott's Whole Hog BBQ became a member of that restaurant family, she made it clear that I was also a member of her family. She's done countless little favors for me—rides, meals, soothing conversations, personal insights—for which I can never thank her enough. More than that, she puts up with Nick's bullshit, and now with my bullshit, too.

So in lieu of the medal that she so richly deserves for all the crucial, thankless, behind-the-scenes work she's done, I offer this, my book, dedicated to her and to all she has meant to this journey.

Thank you, Suzanne Pihakis.

CONTENTS

Snacks, Salads, *and* Vegetables

Desserts

Cocktails

The Pantry

INTRODUCTION

I like spreading the joy and sharing the love, and whole hog barbecue is my means of doing it.

The happiness I get when people are enjoying my food is one of the best feelings I can imagine. That's what I'm thinking about at 2:00 a.m. when everybody else is sleeping and I'm out in the cold night air firing a hog. I'm thinking about how good it's going to feel to see the smiles on people's faces as they eat my barbecue.

I've always imagined being able to cook for people all over the world. I've been lucky. In the past few years, I've had the chance to cook in Australia, Belize, Colombia, France, Uruguay, and all over the United States.

Whenever I cook at a festival or event anywhere in the world, people come up to me and ask for advice on cooking a hog. I'm glad to share whatever information I can, but you can't really teach somebody how to cook a hog in a ten-minute conversation. And you can't go home with everybody and see what they are doing wrong, or doing right for that matter. So it made sense to put what I know in a book and give people all the details and information that I have to share.

The other thing is that if you want to know how to cook a hog right, you also have to know how *not* to cook a hog wrong. I had an advantage. I grew up in it. I saw my father and my great-uncle doing it for years before they let me do it on my own when I was eleven. I had years of my father telling me to be careful about this or don't do that. You can't boil those years down into a quick conversation.

Most of the people who come up to me are backyard cooks. They're mostly men who want to invite friends and family over, pull some good meat off the pit, and have a good time. To do that, you don't just need skill, you need confidence, too. You need to know that when you pull this hog off in 10 or 12 hours, it's gonna be done; it's gonna be done right, and people are gonna be having a good time and laughing with you and not having a bad time and laughing at you.

I've been doing this thirty years. Even now I'll get nervous cooking for a big event or for some famous chef—or even for regular people. One of my faithful customers sent me a text the other day saying she was about to eat the leftovers from the holiday turkey she'd bought from us. I got nervous, wondering, "Is it still gonna be good a few days later?"

When Anthony Bourdain came to interview me for his TV show, *Parts Unknown*, I started off nervous. Then we sat down and talked and it was like we were a couple of old friends. That's the feeling you want to have when you're sharing barbecue.

Relaxed. Chill.

Once you have that confidence you can enjoy the cooking almost as much as you enjoy the eating.

One year, when I was cooking at the Big Apple Barbecue Block Party in New York City, a journalist asked, "What should people expect when they come to your booth?" I told her, "If you're going to be within ten feet of me, be ready to party. If you have negativity, stay out ten and a half feet. Because I'm going to bring you the joy and the fun and I'm going to bring you the best food that I can cook." She laughed and printed that up. And it's true.

The Block Party was an event that Danny Meyer and the Union Square Hospitality Group used to throw every year in Madison Square Park. They'd invite pitmasters from different barbecue regions to come and cook one weekend during the summer. Lower Manhattan is a long way from Hemingway, South Carolina, where my style of cooking comes from. But every year, folks were lined up to groove to the music we played, enjoy the food we cooked, and share the spirit we brought.

This passion for music goes back to my childhood. Being an only child, music was my company, my plaything. I got my first stereo when I was like seven or eight years old. Getting dressed for school in the morning, getting undressed for bed in the evening, and any other time I could squeeze in between I'd be playing music on my stereo. Mostly it was whatever tapes someone had given me. Maybe the Isley Brothers' *Harvest for the World* album or their *Showdown* album with the single "Groove With You" on it. Or I might have been listening to Teddy Pendergrass, who was raised in Philadelphia but who was born just up the road from Hemingway in Kingstree. "The Whole Town's Laughing at Me" was his big hit then,

and I wore it out. Music kept me company then and even now, when I'm cooking late into the night, a lot of times all I have to keep me company is the music.

Music is like an automatic attitude adjustment for me. The songs that I play help put me in the right frame of mind. They remind me of how lucky I am to be able to earn my living by feeding people and making them happy.

I feel like my attitude is my success. My optimism is my success. This outlook allows me to walk into the smokehouse every day and cook the food that people enjoy. Food that people come back for. Food that gets written about around the world. Barbecue that wins awards.

This wasn't always my philosophy. I've been through my share of setbacks. When I started talking about opening my own place in Charleston, my father and I came to a parting of the ways. I couldn't wallow in that though, so I decided to make myself an optimist. My daily outlook became, "Every day is a good day. If I'm still alive, I have a chance." I made the conscious decision not to have any more bad days, only challenging days. Only days that pushed me to be a problem solver. But not bad days. Not ever.

When people ask, how are you doing? I tell them, "I'm great." It's not just something to say. I say it with genuine spirit. With a smile. They say, "but you just went through this, that, and the other." And I tell them, "Yeah, but I'm good. If you didn't find yourself listed in the obituary part of the paper this morning, you won!"

One of the great things about cooking whole hog is that it takes so long to do it, that you just naturally gather around the pit with good friends and fellowship while the meat and wood do their thing. This book is all about inviting you into that fellowship. Once you put these recipes to use, you'll officially be one of us.

"You have to work for what you get"

I don't know if my mother said that to me in the delivery room, but every day of my life after that, if she wasn't saying it, my father was. That was the family philosophy in one word: work.

As a kid, I always felt like I was being singled out. I was an only child, so I didn't have brothers or sisters to compare myself to. But growing up, I always thought that I had a lot more chores to do than any of my friends at school. The Scott family has gotten known for barbecue, but my father always had several businesses going on—the store, the barbecue, the farm, the pool hall, the wood cutting, and even a car repair. For generations the Scotts as well as the Wilsons, my mother's people, have been like that. They always wanted to own something of their own and they didn't care how hard they had to work to get it and keep it going.

When I hear people say "All work and no play makes Jack a dull boy," I laugh. My father is a man of few words. He didn't need all ten of those words to explain how he was raising his son. "All work and no play. Period." At least that's how it felt a lot of the time.

Looking back on it, I realize I'm a lot like my father. Don't get me wrong. I don't believe in being hard on my son or myself in the same ways he was hard on me. I make sure fun time and family time are priorities in my house. But a lot of my drive and success go right back to the way Ella and Roosevelt "Rosie" Scott raised their baby boy.

The way it's supposed to work is this: Once you get to be a man and have a kid or two of your own, you're supposed to crack open a couple of beers with your old man and talk about how it was back in the day, and about how this new generation ain't the same. At that point you're closer to your father than you've been since the days you were a boy and you thought he was the one who set the sun in the sky.

I'm at that age now. So it's difficult that my father and I basically don't speak. That's been the situation for several years now. When it all went down, it rocked my world so thoroughly that I could hardly speak about it. People

would ask me about my childhood or how I learned to cook from my father, and I'd say a lot about the past. But if anyone asked me about the current situation, I'd avoid saying much. A lot of water has passed under the bridge. I like to think of myself as looking forward, as moving forward. But sometimes it helps to look back to understand a thing.

My parents are both from the Pee Dee region of South Carolina. My mother was born in Nesmith. My father was born in St. Mark. Though the towns are only ten miles apart, my parents didn't meet each other in South Carolina. I was curious about that, and one day a friend of mine showed me an article William B. Scott and Peter M. Rutkoff wrote in the South Carolina encyclopedia online: "Between 1917 and 1923, almost half of the African Americans leaving South Carolina went to Philadelphia, and by 1930, 10 percent of the city's black population had been born in the Palmetto State." My parents didn't move to Philadelphia until the 1960s, but they were still following a trend.

My mother had seven sisters and three brothers who survived childhood. Four died young. My mother's father, Jack Wilson, owned his own farm. He didn't want his children working on anybody else's land. Other people would work his kids too hard, he said. He made them work hard, but in the hottest part of the day, he'd send them back to the house. He knew his kids wouldn't get that kind of consideration working for somebody else.

What I remember about Grandaddy Jack is that he used to always have a plug of Red Man chewing tobacco in his mouth. And he had this old paint can that he used to spit in so he could chew his tobacco in the house. He'd tell me or one of my cousins, "Boy go put some dirt in my spitcan," and he would say it just like that, like "spitcan" was one word.

I also remember he would always sit near the door at church. People have said that he'd be packing a pistol right there in the sanctuary, but I never saw it on him.

My Grandmother Ella used to keep Nestlé Nesquik Strawberry powder mix on her table all the time for me and my cousins. And she used to can fruits and vegetables—peaches and succotash I remember mostly.

By the time my mother got out of high school, there wasn't enough work on that little farm to go around. So my mother followed two of her sisters who had already moved to Philadelphia. They lived in North Philly, but they went to Rising Sun Baptist Church in South Philadelphia. My mother remembers it being on 2nd and Washington, but it was really on 3rd and Washington, according to the records I found. To earn a living, my mother sold food at a hospital for a while and she also sewed military uniforms. She has good memories of cheesesteaks and hoagies, but she came home every Christmas—and in our part of the country, Christmas pretty much means barbecuing a hog. I know she had to miss that taste.

My father had jobs at first, then he started his own business, moving furniture. I guess like attracts like and, with all those South Carolina people up there, they naturally gravitated toward each other. He met my mother at the house of a woman named Dorothy Graham. Once they were married, they'd come back to South Carolina several times a year.

In Philadelphia, my mother says, they used to go to parties and concerts. She remembers going to see James Brown and Ike and Tina Turner—Southern singers. What else would you expect from Southern folks living so far from home? My mother had me in November 1971. One month later, they packed up and moved back South for good. All I remember her saying was that she was getting out of the city. After one of those hot days out working in the tobacco fields, I asked her, "So the only place you could bring me to was this farm?"

When my parents first moved back, my father was working at a tobacco warehouse in Winston-Salem. He would go up there on Sundays, work the week, and drive back Friday nights. I don't know if he was planning on buying a store all that time or what, but he saved his money and in 1972, he and my mother bought the business that would become Scott's Variety Store. Along the way, they also bought some farmland. For money, we grew soybeans, corn, and tobacco. In our own garden, we had cucumbers, sweet corn, collards, sweet potatoes, okra, squash, and some sugarcane we grew to make syrup. And of course, we also raised hogs.

In addition to the store, my father had a garage and filling station. He sold regular gas and high-test gas. (Anybody remember high-test gas?) If you needed to change the tires or the oil or the belts on your car, he could do that, too.

Down the road from our store, there was another store and they sold barbecue once a week. That's probably where my father got the idea from to expand our business. My father's uncle, Thomas Scott, was the pitman at first. He'd cook the pig and make the sauce every Thursday when they sold barbecue. One week, he said he was sick and couldn't make it. So my mother made the sauce and my father cooked the pig. They never looked back.

Now all this time, I'm six years old and doing some of everything. I'm sweeping up at the store, putting drinks in the cooler, and fetching wood for the barbecue. There were times when I remember relaxing on Saturday and watching cartoons. But there were also a lot of Saturdays when I was working. The main work I remember then was driving the tractor. You wouldn't believe that they'd have a little kid drive the tractor, but in the country it's like that. Ain't no sitting around. When you' old enough to walk, you' old enough to work.

At the height of our family's farming we had eleven fields of tobacco. That doesn't include the feed corn and soybeans and cucumbers and watermelon and other stuff we'd grow commercially. And it doesn't include the vegetable garden where my mother grew a few things for us to eat. Of all the things we grew, the one I hated the most was tobacco. But in Carolina tobacco was king of the cash crops, so we had to grow it. It took a lot of workers to get a crop out of the field. By the time I was ten or eleven, I'd be involved in pretty much the whole process of harvesting the tobacco.

You'd start harvesting tobacco in late June. Around 6:00 a.m. we would take our pickup truck and pick the workers up from their homes. There might be eight or ten people sitting in the bed of that truck by the time we had everybody. Early in the morning, it was still cool, but there was so much dew on the tobacco leaves that you'd get wet picking it. Then by midday the sun would come up and you'd be even wetter with sweat. In the field, every fifth row was wide enough for the tractor, or harvester to drive down. You would harvest four rows at a time, the two closest to the harvester and the two just on the other side of those. The people harvesting the far rows would sit on these long poles that would extend out from the harvester. The four people picking tobacco would look for the mature, yellow leaves at the bottom of the plant. The young, green leaves at the top don't cure well. The brown leaves weren't any good either. So you had to harvest every row several times as more leaves became ready.

The croppers were usually men. Once they had picked three or four leaves, they would hand them up to the stringers, who were usually women. The stringers would tie the leaves together and then tie them on sticks. There would be a metal dray behind the tractor and the stringer would throw the sticks back there once they were full. The tractor moved slow, but it never stopped until it got to the end of a row. Then you might get a few seconds rest while it turned to go down the next row. You had to drive the tractor straight, otherwise the croppers on one side couldn't reach the plants and the croppers on the other side would be in the middle of the leaves. From time to time you would hear the croppers yell "Get over!" and the driver would have to straighten it up. You would do this all day until lunchtime.

Lunchtime was interesting because it could vary so much. Some days lunch would be pork and beans and rice and some bologna. Or it could be a slice of cooked bologna or luncheon meat on a sandwich with a soda. Some days you didn't leave the fields. They would go get a pack of bologna and a loaf of bread, a pack of NABs cookies, those six-in-the-pack snacks that Nabisco made. Since lunch would be a couple of hours, some people would go home and eat. Other people would eat in the field and find a shade tree to take a nap. If we were lucky, my mother might cook something at the store or at the house, and we'd have fried pork chop sandwiches or something good like that. Then back to work.

A couple of the fields were right by the house, but some were four or five miles away between Hemingway and Nesmith. Sometimes we would work several fields in one day. The workers would finish around 6:00 in the evening and we would drive them all home. But me, being the owner's son, I had to stick around long after everybody else was at home. Then I'd help hang the tobacco in the barns to cure. I might not get home until 8:00 or 8:30 that night.

The next morning, we'd get up around 4:00 a.m. My mother would make breakfast—usually bacon, eggs, and grits. We'd drive to the tobacco barns and take out the sticks of tobacco that had been curing for several days, and load them into the truck, then drive them to the pack house, where we'd store them until time to sell them. This would go on until August or September when the last of the leaves were ready to pick.

Usually, we sold our tobacco in Lake City. On sale day, farmers from all around would bring their tobacco to the warehouse. The men from the tobacco companies would walk from aisle to aisle bidding on each lot. We were kids, so we had to keep out of the way. But sometimes we might see the name of a major cigarette company attached to the tag on our tobacco. That way you knew down the line that your tobacco was going to become a Winston or a Marlboro or a Lucky Strike cigarette.

I hated farming. There's not a damn thing I miss about it. I hated going out early in the morning. I hated having to work in the sun all day. Maybe I didn't understand the importance of farming, but I didn't like it at all. A lot of people marveled at the fact that I cooked all night, several nights a week for more than twenty years. But they don't know the deal. Compared to farming, barbecuing hogs is easy work.

If I wasn't farming, I was doing chores around the house or the store. I had a cousin or two who worked as hard as I did. But I also had a cousin or two who would tell their parents that they didn't want to come by our house because of all the work they would have to do. You couldn't blame them. We'd be out in the field most of the day cropping tobacco or pulling potatoes or something like that. Or, we'd be cleaning up around the store or cutting grass or something.

There were some good times mixed among the work hours.

Sometimes me and my father would be driving back from the fields and he'd ask me if I wanted to pull over and drop a line in the water, see if we could catch a fish. Half the time we wouldn't fish long and we wouldn't catch any fish. But sitting there, my father was relaxed, and so I could relax and enjoy the moment.

My father also had a motorcycle when I was a kid, an old Honda. One of my big thrills was when he would pick me up and ride me on it. We kept our hogs next to my maternal grandmother's house. So we might ride over there to feed the twenty or thirty hogs we had. Or he might pick me up from the store if I'd been spending the day there with my mother. He'd ride with me in front of him, me holding on to the gas tank as we headed home. I would lean down sometimes, then I would lift my head up, then lean back down. You would swear that I was the one driving that thing and I was going fast, fast.

My mother wasn't a motorcycle rider, but we had fun riding bikes. My first bike was a yellow Huffy. Then I got a burgundy ten-speed. My mother would take the old Huffy and we would ride bikes in the sand together. She really must have loved me to do the hard work of peddling through that sand.

On Sundays, she and I would go riding in her old Plymouth to visit relatives or drive around just to get out of the house. Mama wasn't like me. She wouldn't have the radio blaring, but she did love her some Otis Redding. One of those Sundays we were driving and "(Sittin' On) The Dock of the Bay" came on and my mother reached down, gentle as you please, and turned the volume up just a little bit.

In the summer of 1983, NASA conducted its first night launch of a space shuttle. The Space Shuttle Challenger would take off from the Kennedy Space Center in Florida and it would be visible as far away as North Carolina and Virginia. That meant we should have been able to see it in Hemingway. There was another reason we were excited about this launch. Gary Bluford was going to be the first African American and the second Black man ever to go into space. (I didn't know it then, but the Afro Cuban cosmonaut Arnaldo Tamayo Méndez flew on the Russian Soyuz spacecraft in 1980.)

Me and my mom turned up the TV so we could hear the countdown. Then we went outside to see the shuttle. We looked around and we looked around, but we didn't know exactly what direction to look. At the very last second, my mama hollered, "Look at it! There it go. Right there!" That's a moment I won't forget.

In addition to those good times, my mama taught me something that they should put on a billboard in every county in every state: "Manners will take you where money never will." She told me that every time I left the house for a school field trip. I always

thought that was the craziest thing. Then I grew up and I realized that a simple "yes ma'am" or "yes sir" was respected much more than a $20 bill. That never escaped me.

"Take your hat off when you eat" and "Wipe your feet before you go into people's house." All that was drilled into me from a young age. She also taught me to be neat and clean. I was washing and ironing my own clothes in grade school, and I still try to look presentable at all times, even when I'm casual or in work clothes.

I like to show people respect. In turn, I hope they extend respect to me as well. This point of view is especially helpful in the management of the restaurant. The way I see it is nobody works *for* me, everybody works *with* me. My older employees are usually mister or miss, like Mr. G in Charleston, and we have two men I call Mr. James, one in Charleston and one in Birmingham.

Maybe my mother was giving me the same advice any mother would give any child in case they might need it out in the big, wide world. Or maybe it was my mother's particular intuition that one day I might make a name for myself beyond our corner of the Pee Dee region of South Carolina. But there is one incident from my young days that seems really important now that I look back on it.

A lot of my mother's siblings moved to Rochester, New York, back in the 1960s. When I was a kid we would drive up there to visit them almost every summer. One year, on our annual visit—I must have been about seven years old—Jimmy Carter was president and he was in town holding some kind of event. We happened to be downtown when he was speaking. I could hear his voice clear as a bell, but I couldn't see him. I tried to peep over and around people, but nothing worked. And I told myself that one day I wanted the world to see me *and* hear me. Much later, I realized I could do that through food. I never imagined the success I'm having now. My dream was to possibly see the world and to possibly be in charge of the family business and let the world know who I was. It feels good now to be living in a reality that's bigger than my old dreams.

Cars Versus Hogs

I cooked my first hog when I was eleven. It's true. But that says more about my father's attitude toward work and play than it says about me being a pig prodigy. I was in middle school and there was a basketball game that night that I wanted to go to. My father told me that if I wanted go to the game, I had to finish all my work first, and my work that day included firing the hog. Then he left.

Every 10 to 15 minutes, I had to put coals under that hog. It was daylight, but it was dark under the pig, even with the coals burning red. I had to keep taking my flashlight and peeping under it to make sure the meat wasn't burning. What I didn't know was that my father had another guy around watching to make sure I kept up. I found that out later. That man didn't do anything while I was cooking. All afternoon, wasn't nobody burning the wood and working the pit but me.

I'll never forget how golden brown the color was on that hog when my father came back. They flipped the hog over and I was like, "Wow. I can do this." But it wasn't like that was the start of a whole new set of responsibilities for me. I still was a helper, not a pitmaster. But I have to give my father credit; he probably knew I was ready because I had been watching him for years by then. And I wasn't just watching; I was always asking questions. I was learning.

In the beginning, my father only cooked one hog, one day a week, on Thursdays. The pit was built kind of low, maybe 2½ or 3 feet off the ground. I was always trying to see what was going on, especially with the fire. And they were always warning me not to get too close. These days we have a burn barrel, a 55-gallon drum that we stand up and feed the wood into to create hardwood charcoal. As the wood burns, the embers fall and we scoop those up to put under the hog. Back then, the wood would just be burning in a pile and you would dig your shovel in there to get your coals to put under the hog.

The aroma that came out of that pit was just unforgettable. And the sound of that fat dripping, "Ssss. Ssss," was, too. I kept asking my father and the one or two other men working with him, "What y'all doing?" Little by little, they showed me. And I loved it. That led to more questions, like "When can I do that?" and "Can I hold the shovel?"

At first they cooked during the day, while I was at school. Later, when I was in high school, they would cook overnight because a lot of people wanted to buy the barbecue for lunch, so it had to come off the pit earlier. In those days, I'd be sleeping when they were doing the cooking, so I would only get to see it every now and again, like during the holidays. Sometimes there would be more men working with my father, and sometimes there would be friends just hanging around shooting the breeze. That's when I saw there was also a kind of fellowship around the pit. It was a one-of-a-kind experience to be out there with the men cooking.

Besides being around the pit, the two things I enjoyed most in those days were music and cars.

I remember this old guy was telling a story one time and he said, "My radio play so good, you can hear the G string on the guitar." And I was like, "What?" I had no more idea what he was talking about than the man in the moon, but I remember sitting there listening for the G string on my little stereo.

Half the people reading this won't know what I'm talking about, but I grew up in the era of the eight-track tape, when there would be four different songs playing and you hit the button to hear the one you wanted to hear. My first tape was Kool & the Gang, "Celebration." I always knew which song was on which program. I would just sit there and push the buttons for hours.

I tell you something else most folks these days don't remember. You used to get in your car and turn the key in the ignition backwards. That way, instead of turning the engine on, and burning all that gas, you would just be able to listen to the radio and turn on the lights. I could sit in the car forever like that, but eventually, I'd hear my mother or father hollering, "Boy, shut that car off. You gonna kill the battery." I'd shut the car off, but next chance I got, I'd be right

back there doing it again. My two favorite things, cars and music. Even now, taking a long highway drive in my truck with the music cranked is almost like a vacation for me. Anthony Hamilton, Maze, The Whispers, The O'Jays, Leela James—these are some of the artists I like to play on the road. I can get a lot of thinking and relaxing done on the road. What could be better than that?

Back in the day, my father didn't believe in foreign cars. But this older guy—we used to call him Pimpy—had a Nissan 300ZX. Sometimes he would let my friend Wayne drive it and naturally he'd call me up and say, "I got Pimpy's car. Let's go for a ride." That was one of the first cars that would talk to you and say things like, "Your lights are on," or whatever.

I would tell my father all the time, "I want a car like Pimpy got!" Then in March of my senior year in high school, my mama told me I had to make a delivery. I got ready to load everything in her car and she told me to hold on. A little while later, my father pulled up in that 1985 Nissan 300ZX, 5-speed.

It. Was. For. Me!

You talk about a kid in a candy store! It was black with a T-top and gold honeycomb rims. When my dad got it, the engine was blown, so he had a new one put in it. It wasn't an old car, but it had been put through its paces. About three or four weeks after I got it, the clutch burned out. Then the timing belt popped and it took two months to get that fixed. That didn't matter to me, though. I loved it.

There were a couple of guys who'd bought Mustang LX 5.0s. Those cars were hot back then. I'd drag race them from time to time on this long stretch of road. We'd line up next to each other and yell "Go!" I'd take the lead early and hear him back there screeching and fishtailing. But a few seconds later, that Mustang would gain traction and go. He'd catch up with me and then pass me. But when he passed

me, I was only in second gear. Around the quarter-mile point, when he *thought* he'd won the race, I'd shift into third gear and my rpm's would shoot up. If he was dumb enough to keep going, I would tear his ass up! He didn't have the power he thought he had. That happened three or four times. Twice to the same dude. But one time, I stretched all the belts on my car, trying to win a race.

My next car was a 1989 300ZX. It was about two years old when I got it and it was candy apple red. I put honeycomb wheels on it, too. Then I got a 1993 pearl white 300ZX, my first new car and my last two-seater. I drove that until about 2003. By then I was preparing to get married and I knew a two-seater wasn't exactly a family car. One of my uncles had a Chevrolet Avalanche and it felt so good and so roomy that I knew my next car would be a pickup truck. For years, I'd always had a pickup truck for work. I'd make sure to keep them clean and I'd put custom wheels on them, but I'd never considered having it as my main vehicle. But seeing that a truck could be comfortable and even luxurious made me look at this in a whole new way. I drove a 1500 GMC Sierra Denali for years. Then I stepped up a notch. Today, I drive a GMC Denali HD 2500 and I love it.

Besides fast cars, my other hobby was fast motorcycles. Maybe that's because some of the best times I ever had as a kid involved being with my father on his old Honda. I remember it had an orange and black gas tank. I knew then, when I got big, I was going to buy me a motorcycle, too. When I was twenty-three, I got my first Honda, a CBR F2-600. My riding partner was Donald "Dr. Love" Smalls. We used to cruise the strip in Myrtle Beach. Eight years later I got a Honda 954-CDR. That was a beast. It weighed almost four hundred pounds. I loved it, but I found that I never had time to ride it. It was foolish to pay insurance and upkeep on a machine that was gathering dust. So I sold it.

I didn't just love to drive cars; I loved to work on them, too. That was always one of my hobbies. So when I was a senior in high school, I applied to an automotive body shop trade school in Nashville. I wanted to do body and fender work because I wanted to create unique vehicles that stood out. I wanted people to see it and say, "There goes Rodney." I got accepted to the trade school, but I was afraid to tell my dad I'd gotten accepted. I knew what he thought: that I was supposed to stay working with him and doing the same thing I'd always done—chopping wood, working at the store, and cooking barbecue.

My parents would talk about school sometimes, but they didn't put a lot of emphasis on it. "Get your lesson." That's how my mother would put it. But schoolwork was secondary to "real work." If I didn't do my homework at school, I might have a little chunk of time I could squeeze in late at night or on the way to school in the morning to finish up. I think my parents knew education was important, but they didn't really understand why. You could see the benefit of hard work—whether it was tending crops or maintaining your business—right in front of your eyes. You would have a bigger harvest or sell more pork or the new paint would look good on the building. But what was the benefit of education? I don't think they really had an answer, so they didn't ask the question. Besides, for Black folk, education didn't necessarily lead to opportunity.

I was a decent student. I made mostly B's and C's. But there was that D I got in math my junior year. They wanted to make me repeat a year in school. Rather than do that, I went to summer school. And, since I was going to summer school anyway, I decided to take a couple of extra classes so my load would be light when I returned to my senior year in the fall. Apparently it was too light for Betty Sue McAlister, the school librarian. Miss McAlister had me in the library during my free periods learning about the card catalog and reading magazines. Even when I graduated, she took the extra step of keeping up with me. "Be humble and stay Rodney," she used to say. And even years later, when I started to get some publicity for my food, she made sure that the local paper took notice.

Betty Sellars, my high school math teacher, is another unforgettable influence. She cared as much about what we did outside the classroom as in it. She'll still send me a sweet message every now and again, telling me she's proud of what I've become.

Debra Wallace taught home economics. Ronnie Woodberry and I were the only two boys in that class, but I swear we didn't just take it to meet girls. Me, I took it because I had taken it in junior high and thought I would enjoy it. My mother had already taught me some basic sewing skills, and Miss Wallace was impressed by that. But my big accomplishment in her class was when me and Ronnie learned how to make pigs in a blanket. You would have sworn that we had made duck à l'orange or something! We were proud.

One semester I made the honor roll. All the other students would be rushing to get to the front of the lunch line when the bell sounded, but if you were on the honor roll, you got to skip to the front whenever you got there. That felt good. But at that point, in ninth or tenth grade, I didn't really have any ambition. The word "career" was scary for me. The guidance counselors would come around and discuss our futures with us and one of their questions was "What do you enjoy doing?"

To put it in perspective, my dad dropped out of high school in the tenth grade. He never really said a lot about what he expected me to do after I graduated. He had a strict mentality: This is where you're going to be; I have plenty of work for you to do around here.

Then you had to consider that by the time I was in junior high school we had gone from cooking one hog a week on Thursday, to cooking two hogs on Thursday. By the time I finished high school, we had graduated to cooking hogs on Friday and Saturday, too. So I was more needed in the business than ever before. Going from one hog a week to three wasn't a ton of extra work. But going from one hog a week to as many as ten a week was a big change.

I remember my high school graduation day. It felt good, walking across the stage with my classmates. After the ceremony, I came out to greet my parents. Without missing a beat, my father said, "You got to cook hogs tonight."

I remember standing in front of the pits that night watching my classmates passing by. In a small town, you recognize every car that passes. So I knew who was going where. One or two people would stop by and speak. Then they would go on to the party and leave me working.

From graduation up until my early twenties, I was confused about what I was going to do. I used to say I was going to leave Hemingway and do something different. After a while, it felt like I was lying to myself. I knew I was going to stay in the business. I hated it until I loved it.

Hating the Holidays

Monday mornings, the pits got cleaned. We took a rake and hoe and cleared out all the ash that had gathered from the previous week's cooking.

Tuesday morning, we chopped down trees in the area, mostly my favorite, oak, but also a lot of pecan and hickory as well.

Wednesday morning, that wood had to be chopped into the smaller pieces that we could fit into the burn barrel.

Wednesday afternoon was nap time.

Wednesday night, we started cooking. About 10:00 p.m. we'd prep the hogs and start the fire.

Wednesday at midnight, we put the hogs on the pit.

Thursday morning, a few hours before noon, we'd flip the hogs, crisp the skin, sauce them, and pull the meat so it would be ready to be sold.

Thursday afternoon was nap time.

Thursday night, we started again. About 10:00 p.m. we would prep the hogs and start the fire.

Thursday around midnight, we put the hogs on the pit.

Friday was like Thursday.

Saturday was like Friday except we didn't cook that night.

Sunday was rest and usually church.

This was basically my schedule for twenty years. I couldn't ask anyone to work that hard now. But when you live it and you don't think about it, it just becomes normal.

The base of the old smokehouse was cinder block. The blocks extended up about four feet. The rest of the structure was wood. We were just a few yards back from the highway and that presented real problems when it rained. Because the highway had been built up above the level of the land, a bad rain meant water would rush from the road right through the smokehouse. The water would be ankle deep and that would happen at least ten or twelve times a year. If the weather was bad, you still had to get out there and cook. Fewer people would show up maybe. But you definitely had to keep cooking. My dad was that kind of guy. "Storm don't stop nothing. People still gotta eat," he would say.

We tried all kinds of things to stop it. Finally we figured out the best place to dig a ditch to divert it and we set up a sump pump to pump it. out. When it rained hard like that you had to make sure that the wood was stacked up high in the burn barrel so the fire would stay roaring. Keeping a fire going in the rain, ain't so bad. Starting a fire with wet wood in the rain would have been a disaster.

A few years ago, I was cooking at Dockery Farms in Cleveland, Mississippi, with the FatBack Collective (you'll read more about them later). Just after we got our fire started, a tornado passed through a few miles away. We didn't get hit by the tornado, but the wind and rain were so strong that it flooded the pits. We didn't know what to do. Nicholas Pihakis, the son of my business partner, Nick Pihakis, came up with a brilliant idea. We took some metal garbage can lids and shoveled hot coals from the burn barrel onto the lids. They floated above the water and maintained the heat under the hog. Genius! Out of that near disaster came one of the best hogs that I ever cooked.

In Hemingway, we always had at least two people out working the pits for security reasons if nothing else. If you were alone, in the middle of the night, in a rural area, anything could happen. But, even with somebody else there working, there was never a time where you could just take a real break and get some real sleep. So we invented tricks for getting a little nap in. For example, you can take a wheel-barrow and turn it into a makeshift La-Z-Boy chair by putting the handles on the ground. The natural design of the wheelbarrow makes it like a recliner. In the winter, you'd add a shovel full of warm coals close to your feet and another pile of coals on the other side to keep your back warm. By the time the coals burned out, the cold would wake you up and you knew it was time to fire up the hog again.

In comparison, cooking in the winter in Birmingham or Charleston at the restaurants feels like a luxury to me now because I have walls around me. I'm secure. The firebox is inside, along with everything else I need, so I don't have to go outside in the dark to get more coals from the burn barrel, for example. It's a lot more relaxing.

When I say we used to cut our own wood, sometimes folks think I meant we went out into the forest and just started chopping down trees. That did happen on occasion, but most of the time when we were out getting the wood, we were helping with a tree that was in the way of someone building an addition to their home. Or sometimes, they were trying to turn a tractor around in the field and a tree was in the way. If there was a big storm that hit the area,

we'd get a lot of people calling us to cut down trees that had blown over or died. Or sometimes loggers who had trees left in an area they had cut would have us come out and clear those.

I was seventeen when I started cooking full time. It took a couple of years for me to stop seeing it as just drudgery and to start actually liking the work, or at least some aspects of it. I always had my music playing. That would keep me company and also encourage some folks to stop by if they were out late. Mostly those would be the party people who were just leaving the club. Come winter, though, it'd get quiet. Folks might show up or they might not. A few people would stop by just to enjoy the heat of the fire box and we'd have like a fireside chat. Then you had your early risers who would come hang out because

they woke up early and didn't have anybody else to talk to. All that made those hours leading up to sunrise a little more pleasant.

But when I was in my late teens and twenties, I wanted to be at the club with everybody else, not sitting in front of a barbecue pit hosting an after-party. Since we didn't cook Sunday or Monday, I had Saturday and Sunday nights. And, being young, I figured that meant I had to go out both nights. I would wake up Monday morning regretting that decision.

The club we used to go to when I was in high school was Studio 261, it was about ten miles from my house on Highway 261. As I got a little older, twenty-four or twenty-five, I'd go to Yesterdays on Myrtle Beach, about an hour away. Then in my early thirties, I kind of settled into a place in Salters called the Night Life. That's where I discovered the Touch Band, an R&B group that plays the hell out of covers. They've been the sound track to much of my nightlife ever since.

With all of those clubs there was a certain amount of driving along dark, two-lane highways to get there and back. You had to be careful to stay sober enough to get home safe. And even if you were stone cold sober, everybody else leaving the club definitely wasn't. My thinking was to get a drink as soon as I got to the club, that'd be around 11 o'clock. Then I'd get another drink right after that. Then I'd drink water for the rest of the night. That way I'd be sober by the time my night was over. Still, I had been drinking earlier in the night and I wouldn't want to have to explain to some policeman that I had been drinking, but I wasn't drunk. Leaving the club, my strategy for not getting pulled over was simple. Because I knew there were only one or two police officers on the overnight shift, my theory was that if I let three or four cars leave the club in front of me, one of those might get pulled over. If so, I would be good. I'm not saying there weren't a lot of holes

in this theory. But, hey, I never did get pulled over. Maybe that was more a matter of my good luck than brilliant strategizing.

For most people, the real good times are around the Christmas and Thanksgiving holidays. You get time off from school or work, you get to spend time with your family or your friends, and you get to eat special meals. For us, holidays meant cooking like a month's worth of food in a week and a half. We still had to do our regular number of hogs. But in addition to that we had to do the special orders of hogs and turkeys. One year, we did eighty hogs. Another year it was more than ninety. (For perspective, remember that we usually did just thirty hogs during a normal week. So holidays could mean roughly three times as much work.)

I hated the holidays.

I still feel like I missed bits and pieces of childhood. From about age 13 to 30, I didn't have what you would call a "real" Christmas. My parents were too busy working and I was too busy working with them. To cook all those hogs and birds, we'd build extra pits outside the smokehouse. So we'd have both sets of pits and two burn barrels going. On Christmas Day, all I did was sleep.

But that didn't work when I started dating. You can't tell a girl that you were up all night cooking and that's why you couldn't bring her a Christmas present. None of her girlfriends were hearing that from their boyfriends, so she wasn't going to accept that from you.

On New Year's Eve in 1999, of course, I wanted to party like it was 1999. But it was a work night. Me and my cousin Barry somehow convinced my dad that we could cook all night long on the 30th and all day long the next day and finish all of our work in time to go to the millennium celebration. We got the hogs off around 8:00 that night. I don't know what Barry did, but I hit the road to get to a club in Columbia two hours away.

I was dressed in a black windowpane suit with red and white stripes. I stepped into the club and I immediately started to get my drink on. By the time midnight came, I don't know what was redder, my suit or my eyes. Everybody was worried about Y2K and the possibility that, since computers were all programmed for years with dates beginning with "19," all hell would break loose the first time they had to process a year in the new century. That ended up being a big nothing. Everybody froze for a second. When the world didn't end, everybody went back to partying. I got home, slept away what was left of that night and some of the next day, then went right back to working.

One thing did change around the time of the new millennium. It was both nothing and everything. I stopped being confused about what I was going to do with my life. The words "supply and demand" and "capitalize" were in my head for some reason. Maybe I'd been reading about them in a magazine. But I started to ask myself, how could I capitalize on my skills and create something for which there would be more demand? I could detail the hell out of a car with my washing and waxing skills, but that wasn't exactly something I wanted to do with the rest of my life. I hadn't gone to auto body school. So I couldn't take car detailing to the next level.

What I could do was cook barbecue. There would always be a demand for food in general and, judging from the people who came to buy barbecue from us, there would always be a demand for the kind of food that I had learned how to make and that took too much time and effort for most other people to ever master.

It wasn't like there was some moment when I saw the light and everything changed. What really changed was my attitude, and that showed in little ways. My parents had taught me how to make the food right, and I had mastered that pretty much like muscle memory. I also started taking a personal pride in doing it well. I might overhear a customer saying it was too spicy or the bread on the sandwich was soggy and I'd start thinking about ways to address those problems in advance and see to it that all our customers were as happy as could be.

Then there was the issue of the place itself. I thought we should try to make it as attractive as possible, so I'd make sure that the yard and porch were swept clean. Then I decided to paint the building, to give it some curb appeal. My mom had a Carolina blue Cadillac at the time. I decided that blue would be a good color. When it came to doing the work, my parents didn't resist, but they did have an attitude like, "Well, if that's what you want to do, go ahead."

There was another area where I did get resistance. My father was always kind of penny wise and pound foolish. He'd rather spend a nickel to fix something every week than spend a dollar to get something new. There was a step leading up to the grocery that was a little rickety. The truth of the matter was, the whole staircase wasn't in good shape. My father wanted to repair the stair; I wanted to replace the staircase. We ended up replacing it.

We had these trailers we would use to haul wood. They were constantly breaking down or needing new tires because one of the axles was bent. One day I said to him, "Why don't we just get another trailer." I almost knew his answer before he said it. "You don't need to be getting something new and having all those payments to make." Working with my father, I felt like I had all the area mechanics on speed dial because I was calling them all the time to fix things.

Way back when I was in high school, we started to have an annual community picnic. The idea was for some of the Black businesses in the area to get together and throw a thank you party for the community. We would serve a lot of free food like barbecued chicken and perloo (pronounced PER-low), the rice dish that's like South Carolina's jambalaya or biryani (see page 122). We'd also sell our barbecue pork. The first two years it was held in October. It wasn't a big success either year and the other businesses started backing away from doing it. The third year, I told my mother that we should move it to the Saturday before Easter. It was a holiday weekend already, so there would be a lot of people around. And even if nobody else came, she had a huge extended family and that was one of the times most of them came back to visit. She agreed and even let me pick the deejay. It was a big success.

After we had been doing it for a few years, I discovered the Touch Band and decided to pay the money for live music. That was an immediate success, so the next year we built a little platform for them to play on. Every year, the platform would be a little weather-beaten and I'd have to repair it before the picnic. Finally one year, I decided to build a real stage. I put up lights, I put a roof over it, and I wired it up so the band would have a place to plug in their instruments. I even put in ceiling fans and a handicap ramp. It was what I call "county legit," meaning we abided by all the rules and regulations of the county government. Still, I would hear grumbling from my father and other people hanging around. "What's he doing all that for?" and "That don't make no damn sense."

I was so certain that it did make sense and that I was doing the right thing to build our business that I didn't pay the naysayers any mind.

In the moment, those seemed like relatively minor disagreements. My father's ideas—whether they were about equipment repairs or community outreach—would save money in the short run and that made sense. My approach would save time and money in the long run. That also made sense. But little by little it became clear to me that our two philosophies could not coexist. Looking back on all these little signs, I can see now that my father and I could not have been in business together for the long haul. But at the time, the thought that we would ever *not* be in business together never occurred to me.

The Mountaintop

It was 2000. I had driven over to Columbia for the weekend. Heading home on the highway, I saw my parents' car heading in the opposite direction. I didn't think anything of it. That's small town life. You pass familiar cars all the time. I got home and I saw a guy I knew. He asked me how my daddy was doing.

How my daddy was doing? What?

He told me he had heard my father had had a stroke and he was wondering how he was doing. My mother didn't have a cell phone then. By the time I finally was able to catch up with her, she confirmed that my father had had a stroke. He'd complained to my mother about real bad cramps in his arms. He went to the doctor, but they'd sent him home without much of a diagnosis. When things didn't get any better, my mother took him to the hospital. They kept him there three or four days.

When he got home, he couldn't get out of the chair or out of the bed on his own. We had to help him with everything. But in time, he could walk a little, then pretty well. He was still favoring his right side, but he got to the point where he could feed himself and even drive, if the distance wasn't too far. Before long he was sort of his old self. He was physically limited, but he was able to supervise the wood cutting and the cooking and tell me, "Too much of this. Not enough of that."

That's when I really had to learn to cut a tree down on my own. I had been around when the trees were being cut down, but my job was to cut them up into smaller pieces after they were on the ground and haul them off. I was scared to cut one down myself and I had a right to be. Tree cutting is one of the deadliest things you can do for a living. A couple of guys working with us had gotten some bad cuts with the chainsaw. Nothing stitches couldn't fix, though, but it easily could've been worse. Twice a falling tree had done minor damage to a house near where we were working. We'd been lucky so far, and that's how I wanted to keep it.

At that time, my job was basically working the pits at night while my father cut wood during the day. With him out recuperating, I didn't know whether to work nights or days. I tried to do both. I fell asleep in the barber shop one day and a man woke me up and said, "I'm proud of you trying to do what you're trying to do. A lot of people would just leave and give up." He didn't know how close

I had come to doing just that a few years earlier. But if I was all in before the stroke, I damn sure wasn't going to abandon my family now.

Bit by bit, we figured out a schedule that kind of took the pressure off. Someone else helped cut the wood. Since I didn't have to get it all, I could come home early in the day and get some sleep before cooking that night.

Not too many years after my father's stroke I met Reggie Gibson, a Charleston architect. That introduction would dramatically alter the course of my life. Nothing about our meeting suggested it would be such a big deal, so naturally I didn't take notes about it. Some of what I'm writing comes from calling him and getting his side of the story after the fact.

Reggie is one of those people who likes to just drive around to different places in different parts of the state and check them out. He's an architect, so when he's driving around, he's looking at buildings. He's also a food guy, so he's always tasting the regional foods. One day he was in our neck of the woods and he asked a woman where he could get something to eat, like at a restaurant. She said she didn't know anything about any restaurants in the area, but she knew the Scotts cooked good barbecue. Once he got to our place, his curiosity lead him to the smokehouse, and naturally he poked his head in, which most customers didn't do. Then he ordered some food, just like everybody else.

Now years before this meeting, we'd been having a problem with smoke in the smokehouse. While our business was smoking hogs, it felt like we were smoking people—we couldn't seem to get the smoke out of the building, and that was making it difficult to work there and breathe at the same time. I found a health department handbook, and it recommended a gable roof to solve problems like ours. The height and shape of the roof would draw smoke up and out. So we tore out the old roof and put in this tall, gable

roof. We screened that in and put an overhang to keep the rain out.

Reggie says that the first time he saw our operation it was a "mystical experience." It was nighttime when he got there, and we were cooking. He saw the burn barrels with the wood embers glowing and the automobile axle stuck in it to keep the big pieces from falling through among the little coals we were shoveling out to cook with. He saw the embers glowing under the pork. He looked up and saw the gable roof. All that knocked him out. And that's what he thought *before* he tasted the meat. As for the meat itself, "It was the best barbecue I'd ever eaten. There wasn't any question," he says.

I remember him coming back two or three times with his architecture students. Looking at the roof was supposed to make the whole thing an educational experience, I guess. But, knowing Reggie, he probably wanted an excuse to get in some good eating while also teaching his students. Over time, we just naturally became friends.

Years later, Reggie was in Las Vegas at a restaurant he had designed for Louis Osteen, a great South Carolina chef who left us way too soon. John T. Edge, the director of the Southern Foodways Alliance, was there because Louis was a founding member of the organization. The conversation went like this: Reggie told John T. that he had "been to the mountaintop." And John T. told him something like "Yeah, yeah, everybody talks about how they have been to the mountaintop and found the best barbecue, and it's usually bullshit." Reggie wouldn't back down. He told John T. that we made the best barbecue he'd ever eaten. Down the road John T. was writing for the *New York Times*. He called Reggie and asked him about us. He wanted to take the trip and taste for himself and maybe write about us for the newspaper.

By that time we had already had some media exposure. *Southern Living* had mentioned us in a piece in 1997. And when the Carolina Panthers played the Green Bay Packers for the National Football Conference title that year, Governor David Beasley bet ten pounds of Pee Dee region barbecue against some Wisconsin cheese. He didn't mention Scott's Pit Cook B.B.Q. by name, but those in the know knew. And we'd gotten a mention in a write-up once when I. S. Leevy Johnson, a South Carolina lawyer, legislator, and funeral home owner, fed some of our barbecue to the celebrity lawyer Johnnie Cochran. But even among folks who knew barbecue, we were not famous.

John T. must have called the store to set up the visit for the story. My conversations with my mom went something like this:

"A guy called. He said he wanted to do a piece for the *New York Times*."

"The *Times*?"

"I don't know. Something. I gave him your number."

I didn't know who John T. was, but I knew the *Times* was a big publication. When he called, I was cutting wood with my dad and I didn't want him yelling at me for being distracted. We had a quick conversation and he told me when he'd be coming out to see us.

When he came out we didn't do anything fancy or out of the ordinary. He spoke to several people. My dad was real quiet. My mom said, "Talk to Rodney." The piece ended with quotes from me and my dad that I still like a lot.

"This is a business for us," my dad said. "We don't do it the old way. We do it the best way we know how. That means a lot of oak. That means a lean pig, which means less grease and less of a chance of grease fires. No matter which way you do it, though, some folks don't want you to go nowhere."

I echoed his feelings. "People keep talking about how old-fashioned what we do is," I said. "Old-fashioned was working the farm as a boy. I hated those long hours, that hot sun. Compared to that, this is a slow roll."

After that article appeared, the phone at the store was ringing off the hook for a while with people calling to say they had read about us in the paper. I sort of became the official spokesperson for Scott's Pit Cook B.B.Q. That seemed just fine with my parents. Neither one of them was really looking for the limelight.

SOUTH CAROLINA

Pork Palaces of the Pee Dee

A local connoisseur leads a safari into Carolina 'cue country.

Buddy Hanna knows barbecue, especially the vinegar-laced variety favored in the Pee Dee. So when the aficionado offers to introduce us to his preferred purveyors of pig, my dog, Tann Mann, and I bark, er, jump at the chance.

Buddy's something of an expert on the pungent pork of his boyhood neighborhood. As his wife, Terri, navigates, Buddy lists the qualities of barbecue particular to the Pee Dee.

• **Heat:** The Midlands likes mustard, but vinegar rules this area.

• **Love:** "Like oyster roasts on the coast, barbecue is what we do here to share community and family." This son of the Pee Dee estimates he's roasted at least 50 hogs himself.

• **Pork:** It's all about succulent pig.

Whole Hog in Hemingway

By the time we pull off State 261, I'm hungry enough to eat, well, a pig. We tumble out of the car at Scott's B.B.Q., a place softly charred by 30 years of roasting hogs.

My belly aches with desire as we order at a window in the rear of the variety store. You can take home the delectable flesh of a whole hog or half a hog, but we have a lot of eating to do in one day, so we settle for meat by the pound. There's no dining accommodation, so I plunk down on the only seat—a pew on the front porch—to sample the ribs. The pork plucks with vinegar and sets my lips asmacking.

"I think it's the finest smoked meat ever; they hand-separate every ounce, so there's no gristle," Buddy raves. No

one fusses with sides here—they just do meat.

The smokehouse behind the store accommodates 14 pits where up to 4,000 pounds of pork smoke every week, low and slow, over split oak. "Other than digging a hole in the ground, this is as authentic as it gets," Buddy opines. "You won't find pig as good as Scott's. That's goood pee-ug." Leave it to Buddy to make "pig" a two-syllable word. ▸

"Other than digging a hole in the ground, this is as authentic as it gets."

Buddy Hanna

First stop on the Pee Dee 'cue safari: Scott's B.B.Q. in Hemingway. Writer Holly Herrick takes the only seat in the house to sample the piquant pork, keeping her dog, Tann Mann, waiting for a tidbit.

Charleston Calling

I said that meeting Reggie helped change my life. Well, the final link of the chain between meeting Reggie and opening up Rodney Scott's Whole Hog BBQ fell into place not long after the *New York Times* article appeared.

John T. called and said that he wanted me to meet this guy.

Next thing I knew, Nick Pihakis came by. I didn't know it then, but Nick had started Jim 'N Nick's Bar-B-Q restaurants, a chain based in Birmingham. He came with Dan Latham, a chef who was working with him at the time. They tasted the pork and then Nick gave me this look like "Wow!"

That's how it all started.

Charleston is about two hours southwest of Hemingway. It's not that far, but it sometimes feels a world away. We didn't go there often. We had other cities that were closer if we needed to go shopping or wanted to party away from home. I certainly had never been to the Charleston Wine + Food festival. So when my new friend Nick Pihakis called and invited me to cook for an event during the festival, I wasn't sure what to think. I wasn't opposed to the idea, but I wasn't jumping for joy, either.

Once I decided to stay in the family barbecue business and not move away and not

work at a body shop, I committed myself to trying to cook the food the best I could. I was proud of that. I was also proud of the fact that in my small town, where so many young Black men fall through the cracks, I had done well. No arrests. No convictions. No addictions. I did have dreams that were bigger than the Pee Dee region. The ambition inspired by that moment of not seeing President Carter was real. But even now, I can't really lay out plainly what my life would have looked like if I had not moved to Charleston and opened Rodney Scott's Whole Hog BBQ. Those dreams of mine were heartfelt, but they weren't specific. There was no plan to get from here to there because I didn't know exactly where "there" was.

When you grow up in a small town in this country, and you don't have the best education, and don't have a lot of money, and you don't have a lot of exposure, people think you've made it if you stay out of trouble and hold down a job. When you add the racial aspect on top of that—and the history of race in this country especially—you can understand what I was dealing with even better. Sometimes I'll be sitting around drinking with my white friends and they tell me some of the things they did when they were teenagers. I say to myself, "If I had done that, they would have put me under the jail, and I would still be there!" I promised myself that I'd never be as hard on my son as my parents were on me. But one reason my parents raised me the way they did was they knew that Black boys often don't get second chances or the benefits of any doubts. The authorities talk to us like that card in the Monopoly game, "Go to jail. Go directly to jail. Do not pass Go. Do not collect $200." Growing up, you spend so much time looking down to avoid the traps and pitfalls that you don't always have the energy to look up and see the horizon.

I remember when I was about thirteen or fourteen and I was just getting ready to get my driving permit. There was an older guy talking to my father and, as I was walking by, he stopped me. He said to my father, "I'm going to tell you right now, right in front of your son. If Rodney gets in trouble and goes to jail, leave him there. Let him learn that ain't nobody just gonna be coming to rescue him when he gets locked up."

When that old man said that, I said to myself, "I'm going to get ahead of you. I'm never going to go to jail." And I've never been to jail. I also asked myself, what else do I need to do to keep out of harm's way. At the top of that list was stay away from troublemakers.

There used be a lot of drugs between Hemingway and Lake City. But there were also a lot of pretty girls and good times in Lake City. Me and my boy Wayne Brown used to go there a lot in high school, and we never had any problem. Years later one of the guys who was kind of on the rough side told me that nobody messed with me and Wayne because there were only two of us. When two teenage boys

are traveling in a pair, they are probably looking for girls, he said. When they travel in a larger group, they're looking for trouble.

I wanted to be a success. And even before I knew exactly what that would mean in my life, I knew that it started by avoiding trouble. Once I got in my thirties and hadn't had any problems with the law, I figured all I had to do was maintain.

Success is defined in so many ways. One way to be successful is to be alive the day after yesterday.

I talked to quite a few people around Hemingway and Nesmith about my dreams and my ambition to make the business grow. Most of them would say, "You're crazy. That's not going to happen." There were one or two people who were genuinely encouraging. They would say, "You should open a sit-down spot," or "Y'all should have a buffet." Then you had the old-school folks, saying "Just remember to keep the Lord first."

A person growing up like I did wants the nice things they see around them—a new car, a beautiful house, a business maybe, a few dollars in the bank. But a lot of the time people in that situation have no real idea of what life can offer. Cooking in Charleston had never been a goal of mine. I never saw that as a stepping-stone to some other thing. So when Nick called me and asked if I wanted to cook for that event, I'm not sure exactly what I said. But I know it wasn't an immediate "Yes."

There was a Jim 'N Nick's in Charleston. The next time Nick was there to check on things, he drove up to Hemingway to see me. I fixed him a barbecue sandwich with crackling skin on top of the meat, and we talked. He explained that his company and the Southern Foodways Alliance, John T.'s organization, were starting a series of pitmaster dinners. Every year, they wanted to feature a different pitmaster cooking a special dinner at their restaurant during the Charleston Wine + Food festival.

That was strange. A barbecue man wants to invite another barbecue man to cook in his restaurant? Why?

Two things you have to understand about Nick Pihakis. First, he's a businessman. He knows what it takes for a business to grow and earn a dollar. Second, he's interested in the culture around food, especially Southern food. This event was about him celebrating the kind of old-fashioned barbecue that made modern barbecue restaurants like Jim 'N Nick's possible. Celebrating another pitmaster wasn't going to hurt his business. In fact, celebrating good barbecue could only help his business. I agreed to go down there and cook.

King Street is one of the most important, most historic streets in Charleston. For this event, Nick got permission to park a huge barbecue rig and burn barrel on the street. It's already a narrow street. We didn't close it down entirely. So cars had to kind of ease alongside of us. A few businesses called the police to find out if we had a permit to be there. But the fire department had already signed off on it, so we were good.

I had never cooked for a big event like this before. It wasn't so much the number of people, it was also the fact that, unlike cooking in Hemingway, I'd be cooking for a bunch of people I didn't know and who didn't know me. I dealt with it by just focusing. "Cook the hog, Rodney. Cook the hog." For a second, when it came time to season the hog, I kind of froze. I'd done it a thousand times, but for a brief second, I was like "Are you sure you know what you're doing?"

Part of my concern was with the flavor profile of our food. I knew how to cook for the people who lived around Hemingway. They were my people. I grew up with them. I wasn't worried about cooking for the people who traveled to get our food. Not to put it too bluntly, but I was on my home turf. If they didn't like it they could go home. But, in a sense, I had been invited into someone else's home to cook. And yes, they invited me after having tasted my food. But that day I was doing a quick check-double-check of my own approach. Then it was like I heard a voice saying, "Just do your thing."

Mike Mills was standing beside me when I started seasoning the hog. I always thought of Mike Mills as a legend. He owns 17th Street Barbecue in Murphysboro, Illinois. He's won the Memphis in May World Championship Barbecue Cooking Contest and other contests several times and he's well known as one of the big dogs in our field. Just his presence made me feel like I had his support. Still, somebody saw I was nervous and brought me some kind of whiskey. Before I could finish it, Julian Van Winkle of the famous Old Rip Van Winkle whiskey brand, came up and said, "Here. Take a real drink," and handed me a generous shot of Pappy Van Winkle. Once again, this man who makes bourbon that people fight over and spend hundreds of dollars on was offering me a taste like I was one of the family. So me and the bourbon got ourselves together and finished the pig. Then a new kind of trouble started.

We were going to walk from the street through the restaurant with the pig on a platter, making a grand entrance. Halfway into the dining room, I got a cramp in my wrist. I said to myself, "Lord, please don't let me drop this hog!" Despite that cramp and the scare, me and the pig made it safely to the kitchen.

The other aspect of that dinner was the debut of a film about us called *Cut/Chop/Cook*. Jim 'N Nick's sponsored a series of short documentary movies that the Southern Foodways Alliance produced about pitmasters. I was the first one honored that way. The film features me, my parents, and some of our customers. You can still see the film online. I had never seen myself talking on TV for that long before. I had done *Making It Grow*, a show on South Carolina public television, but it wasn't the same. As it was starting up, I was thinking, "Do I look right? Am I explaining this clearly? Am I showing them the best of the world I come from?"

When the film and the meal were over I had people coming up to shake my hand and tell me how much they enjoyed it. One person even asked for an autograph. That made me laugh. Here I was just trying to get through this and I ended up having a good time and receiving high praise.

That event really solidified my friendship with Nick. After Charleston Food + Wine, people passed in and out of Scott's barbecue constantly. I was friendly with all of them, but not too many of them became actual friends. Nick Pihakis did. Between cooking for the pitmaster dinner and him driving up to Hemingway from time to time, we developed a real closeness.

I can't say there was one moment that changed everything in our friendship, but one story sticks out in my mind. Nick's wife, Suzanne, was expecting their first child. They had no money and they'd just started the barbecue business. At 5:00 in the morning, Suzanne's water broke. She needed to get to the hospital, but there was no one else who could set up the restaurant for opening. Nick stopped at McDonald's, he bought one of everything on the breakfast menu, then he went to his own restaurant. He got the pits cranked up and the meat put on. Only then, around 10:00, did he bring his wife to the hospital.

Hearing that story told me that Nick wasn't somebody who came from easy money. He had to work for what he got and he understood what work meant. We had that in common and it made it easier to talk to him. I'd pick his brain about the barbecue business and try to get his pointers on how we could improve what we were doing. Before too long, I didn't just need friendly advice. I needed some real help.

Nick on the Case

Nick Pihakis has wanted to be in the restaurant business since he was fifteen years old. He says it goes back to the days when he would visit his cousin in Miami and they would ride their bikes past the Fontainebleau Miami Beach hotel and see the fancy tableside service the restaurant featured. Back in Birmingham, his hometown, he started bartending when he was old enough. He would also go to the restaurant before his shift and work in the kitchen to learn more about food.

In 1985, his father, the Jim in Jim 'N Nick's, retired from the insurance business and suggested that Nick open his own place. They bought a restaurant that had been a pizza joint, but Nick had always loved barbecue, so that's what they decided to cook. Phillip Adrey, a seventy-year-old Lebanese-American man who had worked the pits at Ollie's Bar-B-Q in Birmingham, had semiretired and was working for a friend of Nick's. He agreed to come on board to teach Nick how to make barbecue commercially.

Nick's plan had always been to own multiple restaurants. Thirty years after they opened, there were more than thirty Jim 'N Nick's operating. In addition to that, Pihakis Restaurant Group is also partners in Hero Doughnuts, Little Donkey (a Mexican restaurant chain), and a couple of other restaurant concepts.

When you talk to Nick, he doesn't mention this all at once. But between me visiting him in Birmingham and us hanging out in Charleston and Hemingway, it became more and more clear that if I wanted to learn about the restaurant business, he had the know-how to be a good teacher. He also has a kind of soft-spoken humility when he's giving you advice. He doesn't just come out and say, "Look, fool, you' doing it all wrong!" He says, "If I were you . . ."

He started making little suggestions each time he came out to Hemingway. For example, he suggested that we serve barbecue on Wednesdays in addition to the Thursday, Friday, and Saturday hours we'd grown into. That made sense. More and more people from around the region and from around the country were coming to eat our food, thanks to the *New York Times* article and other things that

had been written about us. The first few Wednesdays were slow. But after a month or so, they were profitable.

We used to put all the hogs on the pit at the same time and pull all of them off at the same time. That's fine if you're one of the early birds who get there while the barbecue is still at its freshest. But what about the people who come by after work and want some barbecue for dinner? They're getting meat that's been off the pit for ten or twelve hours. Nick suggested that we stagger the hogs, putting one on the pit every two hours and then pulling them off of the pit at two-hour intervals. There's no way to make barbecue to order. Whether you're cooking ribs or chicken for a few hours, or a whole hog for half a day, the cook has to start cooking the meat long before the customer has decided to eat barbecue. I think barbecue in general still tastes good long after it's been pulled from the pit, but as a professional chef, I think I have an obligation to my customers not to serve food that's been sitting around too long. The staggered cook solved that problem.

Another Nick suggestion during the early days of our conversations was that I stop staying up all night cooking. I had become the face of the restaurant. My parents had started the business, but they were more comfortable with me being the one who talked to the press. People who read about us or saw us on a TV segment would want to see the man whose name they recognized when they came by. From an operational standpoint, maybe it was better having me supervise the cooking all night, but from a public relations standpoint, there was no question: I needed to be there and be visible.

One day, I was driving back from Charleston with Nick and he up and said, "You aren't charging enough." So I said, "Okay. With all your expertise, how much do you think we should charge?" He said, "I'd at least go up $1 per pound on the meat."

When we got back to Hemingway, I walked right into the building, got up on a ladder with a Sharpie and changed the price. Nick just yelped! He couldn't believe it. One lady said, "I'm glad I already paid for mine." Another woman said, "I knew I should have come a little earlier."

When I got down off the ladder, Nick told me I should have waited at least a few days or given people a warning that the price was going to go up. I told him something the old folks used to tell me, "Wait broke the wagon." If we had had a bunch of computers to reprogram with the new price, or if we had had

a fancy electric sign, it would have taken us a while to make the change. Even Nick had to admit that there were some advantages to the old-fashioned, low-tech approach.

John T.'s article in the *Times* helped wake up the world to the food we were cooking in Hemingway. It did something else, too. It introduced me to the world of barbecue outside my home state.

Danny Meyer, the restaurant genius behind Union Square Cafe, Shake Shack, Gramercy Tavern, and a lot of the other restaurants on any Best of New York list, decided in 2002 that he and his team were going to open a barbecue restaurant. It made sense. He was from St. Louis and grew up eating barbecue. It also made no sense, because everyone thought the pollution regulations in New York City wouldn't allow you to cook real barbecue commercially. He opened Blue Smoke, but he realized that wasn't enough. New Yorkers weren't used to eating a lot of barbecue. In order to promote the food itself, he came up with the idea of a festival where some of the best pitmasters from around the country would come to New York to cook. He called it the Big Apple Barbecue Block Party, and it would eventually become the biggest barbecue event in New York City and one of the biggest in the country. In 2010, Drew Robinson, the chef at Jim 'N Nick's, was going to be cooking, and Nick invited me to hang out with his crew. A year later I was invited to be one of the pitmasters.

I would be cooking with the best of the best. Chris Lilly of Big Bob Gibson Bar-B-Q in Decatur, Alabama; Ed Mitchell from Raleigh, North Carolina; Pat Martin from Martin's Bar-B-Que Joint in Nashville; Kenny Callaghan from Blue Smoke in New York; Sam Jones from Skylight Inn in Ayden, North Carolina; and about a dozen other top-tier pitmasters. Throughout the years, the event got to be like homecoming for the barbecue brotherhood. It was the one time a year you were guaranteed to see friends from across the country, many of them being the pitmasters you most admired.

Cooking at the Big Apple was like cooking on a stage. The streets were blocked off from cars. Your pits came out into about the middle of the street. The other half of the street was where the crowds of people lined up to buy your food. There are two things I like to do in the restaurant business. The first is make sure my food is the best I can make it. The second is to make sure my customers are as happy as I can make them. Cooking at the Big Apple, I had to do both simultaneously and it was easy to lose focus. By the time I cooked at the last Block Party in 2018 (the Block Party was canceled after it outgrew its home in and around Madison Square Park), I had figured out how to balance everything. But it turned out that the challenges of cooking for a big New York crowd were the least of my worries.

While I was in New York in 2011, my second year at the block party, an old problem resurfaced. My father had had some trouble with his state taxes off and on for years. I didn't know much about it because when it comes to his business, my father plays things close to the vest. My parents had an accountant who was negotiating on their behalf. I assumed he was making some progress. Turns out he wasn't.

I got the news that on June 2, 2011, state officials had come in and ripped down my father's business permit because he hadn't been paying taxes. When I got back to South Carolina, one of the first things my father said to me was "Do you have any money?" I gave him a look like, "Really?" He was the one who paid me. He should have known I didn't have anything. Then he told me how much money we were talking about. It was $50,000. His whole attitude was that the state tax officials were lying. He had even tried to reopen after they had shut him down. Which means he got cited again for operating without a license. His explanations were all just balls of confusion. Every one of them involved somebody else not doing what they were supposed to do, and none of them involved him not living up to his responsibilities. My attitude was that if he had been paying his taxes all along there is hardly any way the state would just up and do this.

That's when Nick stepped in.

He called some folks he knew to negotiate with the state. Nick told them that he wasn't even sure if we were making enough money to pay the taxes, and he had a point. In some ways my father was very smart in the way he structured his businesses. He owned the land, so he wasn't paying any rent. He had me and other relatives working for him, so he wasn't exactly paying union wages. As for the wood we used, he was basically trading the labor of cutting down trees for the use of the wood. He didn't expand the days of operation and put more hogs on the pit until he was sure there was pent-up demand for our food.

All of that is great, especially if you are just starting out and need to take every advantage you can to get the business up and running. The problem is my father had been operating in start-up mode for thirty years. There was no real vision for how to professionalize the business. He wasn't saying, "I'm going to do it like this until . . ." His philosophy was, "This is how you do it."

The resolution Nick was able to negotiate with the state required him to give them a check for $679 to cover one month of estimated taxes (they never cashed Nick's check). Then it was agreed that the business would be put in my name. We actually drew up a contract with my father, giving me control of the business. I also decided that I would drive to Florence every month to pay the taxes. That last part ended up being a real education for me. I wouldn't just go to Florence and hand over a check. I'd sit down with the state's accountant and figure out what the taxes should be. So my tax dollars also bought me an education in state tax procedures. In addition to the current taxes I paid each month, I also paid $1,000 a month toward our back taxes.

I doubt my father would ever have allowed some outsider to get in the middle of his finances. Hell, he didn't even let me know what was going on. But given the choice between me working with Nick and closing the business the choice was clear. If it wasn't for that crisis Scott's Pit Cook B.B.Q. would not have survived. And if it wasn't for another immediate change, I might not have survived.

My father was paying me $400 per week. It seems impossible that I could have lived off of that amount of money. But I was living in a small town. Though I had bought a mobile home in 2000, ten years later, I realized I'd agreed to a bad deal. So I moved back in with my parents. I think if I'd gone to my father and asked for a raise, I could've gotten another few dollars a week. But Nick suggested that I double my salary and he was right. If the business couldn't pay me $800 a week and survive, then it shouldn't survive.

It was a really good time to have my salary doubled. It was during all that tax stuff that I met my wife, Shanika. And you know what they say: *RomANCE without finANCE is a nuisANCE*. When we first started dating, I took to calling her Coco. I told her I did that because she was brown and sweet. I also called her that because I'm better at remembering nicknames than I am at remembering names.

In addition to stabilizing things, Nick helped us modernize operations. We had never taken credit cards. My father had a "cash is king" philosophy, both in his business and his personal life. Since he didn't carry credit cards, he didn't have any personal experience with their advantages. We also had never had modern point-of-sale cash registers. We just took in payments and gave the customers their change and counted up the money at the end of the night. But Nick explained that over his decades in business he had seen the ratio of cash to credit

card payments reverse. In the beginning almost no one paid with a card. Now almost everyone does. The credit card companies make money coming and going. As the merchant, we pay them 2.5 to 3 percent of the revenue we get. Then, as the consumer, you pay them annual fees every year and interest every month. I can understand why someone like my father would feel that they were being cheated with this arrangement. But it's more convenient for the customer, especially for people trying to keep track of their expenses.

Even though I owned the business now, my parents still owned the store and the smokehouse. It was only fair that I pay them rent out of the revenues. I went to my father twice, check in hand, to pay him. He refused both times. So I decided that the best way to handle it would be if I paid all their bills. I told my mother to bring me every bill that came in. So for five years, I paid their electricity, phone, insurance, medical, and repair bills. One day, my father told me that he wanted to buy a used truck. I paid $2,500 for the truck and told the seller to be sure to put it in my father's name. I did something similar for my mom when she wanted a car.

Even though I was in charge, my father was the one who had started the business and he was the elder. It was his business and I couldn't just run roughshod over him. I made a point of consulting him whenever I wanted to make small changes. But over the years, I had figured out that while getting permission from him was impossible, getting forgiveness was merely difficult. For example, I got tired of repairing chainsaws. They were crucial to our business and a bad chainsaw could hurt or even kill somebody. A good model cost about $800. Rather than ask my father what he thought, I just bought the damn chainsaw and went ahead about my business.

Mic drop.

End of discussion.

Fire and Out

The first fire happened in 1989 when I was eighteen years old. The grease caught and quickly spread to the wood boards we were using to cover the hogs in the pit. Next thing I knew the whole building was on fire and it was all we could do to just get out of there. The building was pretty much destroyed, and we had to rebuild it.

The next big fire was in 2013. It was a day or two before Thanksgiving. In addition to our usual hogs, we had a few dozen turkeys on the pits that people had special-ordered. Maybe that was part of the problem. We were used to barbecuing turkeys, but that wasn't exactly part of our normal routine. That one little variation might have thrown the guys off somehow. I wasn't there when it happened, but they told me a hog caught fire and then ultimately the flame spread to the gas line that went to the fryer that we used to cook the pork skins. At that point, fire was just shooting out everywhere. We were lucky again. Nobody got hurt, though we lost the main pit for a while. We were actually back cooking the next day because we had an auxiliary shed away from the main pit area and it wasn't damaged.

When I assessed the damage, it was clear that we couldn't just resume cooking like before. We needed to rebuild from the ground up and we needed to rebuild better than before. That's cheaper said than done. I made a back-of-the-envelope estimation that we'd need $100,000 to do it right.

If we had that kind of money lying around, we would have paid our taxes!

Growing up, people in the community would sometimes come together to help each other pick the crops in their fields before the frost hit or before the bugs ate everything. Not only did I see this in action, I was part of it. Neighbors helping neighbors. We had that kind of spirit in the community. But you need more than good hearts to buy quality materials. I didn't fully realize it before then, but I had a community of friends that extended beyond my geographic area.

In 2011, Donald Link from Herbsaint Bar and Restaurant in New Orleans called Nick with an idea. He wanted to compete in the Memphis in May World Champion Barbecue Cooking Contest. That competition is legendary for all the tricks the pitmasters use to produce the tastiest barbecue. They inject the meat with brine solutions, they spritz it with apple juice, they devise special seasoning blends. There was one thing they tended not to do, and that was cook a hog that had been raised well and fed a quality diet. So Nick and Donald assembled a group of chefs, friends, and writers to participate. It became known as the FatBack Collective. We were out to prove that a good pig—well raised and well cooked—could make the best barbecue even without all the exotic techniques some of the competition guys used. I was a member of the collective and joined in the competition. I read about a guy once who said, with all sincerity, that he'd give his left nut to win Memphis in May. Folks are that serious about it. They come every year, trying to take home a prize. This was the first time any of us had competed and we came in third place in the whole hog division.

On top of that, we had bigger ambitions. We wanted to support small local farms that were raising heirloom breed hogs. And beneath that we had some smaller ambitions involving eating, drinking, and having fun with friends. Then something happened that helped us figure out a mission that could have a more immediate impact than the other things we were doing.

In July of 2012, we came together to help rebuild Sam's Bar-B-Q in Humboldt, Tennessee. Sam Donald opened his place in 1988. He passed away in 2011 and his daughter and son-in-law kept the business going. When the building was destroyed in a fire, I got my hands dirty alongside other members of the FatBack Collective doing the physical labor of rebuilding the pit. Little did I know I'd be in a similar position myself a few years later.

When we had our fire, everyone in the collective wanted to help out. It was Nick who came up with the idea of the "Rodney in Exile" tour. The plan was that my friends would host fundraising dinners at their restaurants and I'd cook a whole hog as the main course.

We started in Atlanta at Gunshow, where chef Kevin Gillespie and chef/photographer/food stylist Angie Mosier were the hosts. (Angie has a gen-erous spirit and has stepped up often to help me and a lot of other people.) Then it was on to Husk Nashville with my man Sean Brock, his pastry chef, Lisa Marie Donovan, and pitmaster Patrick Martin. In Oxford, John Currence, Nick Reppond, and John T. hosted us at Lamar Lounge. Then I cooked with those great New Orleans boys, Donald Link, Ryan Prewitt, and Stephen Stryjewski at Cochon. Birmingham is Nick's home turf so we did an event with his chef, Drew Robinson, at a Jim 'N Nick's location. We ended the tour in Charleston with Sean Brock again, but this time my old buddy Sam Jones from Skylight Inn BBQ in Ayden, North Carolina, cooked as well.

Barbecue is such a regional thing that, in addition to folks being kind enough to help me out, they were also getting a chance to taste a style of cooking that they probably could not have gotten in their neck of the woods. That's part of the reason the tour was such a success. The good news is that we raised $80,000. I took $60,000 of that to apply to the rebuild. With that as a jump-start, my family and I decided we'd be responsible for any costs beyond that. We left $20,000 in the FatBack Collective kitty for the next time someone would need assistance (in the barbecue business, it seems like there are only two types of restaurants: those that *have* had a fire and those that *will* have a fire).

During my tour, I'll never forget a small thing that happened in New Orleans. We were sold out and one guy showed up with his lady and asked what was going on. I told him and he turned away from me for a moment, then turned back and gave me a $2 bill. He couldn't even get into the event, but still he wanted to wish me well. All those other dollars we raised have long since been spent. That $2 bill I still keep in my wallet. It's a reminder to stay on top of my game and to keep working so that I don't ever get so broke I have to spend that $2.

When we rebuilt, we decided that we were going to do things differently. The main thing was to use noncombustible metal wherever possible so that even if we did have a fire it would be contained by the material itself. Also metal lasts longer and cleans easier than cinder block. We also poured a new foundation so that we wouldn't have a problem with the pits flooding during a rainstorm.

We made the space a little bigger, too. Used to be that whenever we needed a pig, we could call the locker plant, which was only two miles away, and tell them how many pigs we wanted and they would deliver them the next afternoon. When it came to the holidays, instead of somebody having to deliver to us, they just parked their refrigerated truck on our property. We took out the hogs the next day and they could pick up their truck after the holiday. That's small-town, handshake ingenuity. After the rebuild, we installed a walk-in cooler and added a building that connected the smokehouse to the store where we sold the barbecue. Even now, I take the tricks of the trade that I learned in Hemingway everywhere I go. In Charleston the locker plant will park their refrigerated trucks in our lot rather than force someone to deliver on a holiday when they'd rather be off.

In early 2016, just as things were kind of getting back to normal at Scott's, Nick had another idea.

Our old architect friend Reggie Gibson had done the design for a fried chicken restaurant on King Street in Charleston. That restaurant was going out of business. What if we opened up a whole hog barbecue restaurant in that space?

I thought this was an incredible opportunity. I had all kinds of ideas and dreams about how I wanted to present my food and accommodate my guests. But even I knew that it took more than good food and a big dream to make a successful restaurant. Opening a barbecue spot with Nick presented the chance to work with someone I trusted and who had years of experience doing this successfully. Here was somebody I could trade ideas with until we came up with the right ones. Here was somebody who could walk into a bank and walk out with enough cash to do this thing right, so that I wouldn't end up running out of money before the business was mature enough to support itself.

The idea was that Rodney Scott's Whole Hog BBQ on King Street in Charleston would be a totally separate operation from Scott's BBQ in Hemingway. It seemed to me like a great arrangement. I had rebuilt both the building and the business. We were making more money than ever. Any revenue Hemingway generated would stay there. I was going to step out and leave the business to them. When I told my father, he didn't seem to have a problem with it.

I was high just on the *possibility* of going into partnership with Nick on this new place. But that wasn't all that was going right. The rebuilt pits were cooking at least as well as the ones they had replaced. We'd done good business, which was to be expected. What was a slight surprise is that we started 2016 off so strong. Usually it seems people start the new year off too broke or too fat to want to buy a lot of barbecue. Not that year. If we could keep going at that pace, we would have our best year ever.

There was one problem, though, and it had the potential to be a big one.

My mother was feeling bad. She had her brother drive her to the hospital. My uncle didn't even call to tell me my mother was sick. When I got there, the doctor wanted to talk to me. My uncle tried to step in and say he was the family member the doctor needed to talk to. But the doctor said, "No. I need to talk to her son." He told me that he couldn't find anything wrong with her, per se. He urged me to keep an eye on her and bring her back if need be.

I knew my mother was not at her best. I could see that she was tired. I worried that she wasn't the kind

of tired you can shake off with a night or two of good sleep. I knew that she would have to be low sick to not show up to work. She wouldn't sit at home. She would fight, and that's what worried me.

By then, I'd gotten my third invitation to cook in Australia and that gave me an idea: Why don't we close the restaurant for a week? That way my mother wouldn't have the physical drain of working all day and she wouldn't have the mental drain of thinking about what was going on at work while she wasn't there. Things were going well financially. We could afford to pay everyone for a week and not have a problem. I told my parents my plan. I tried to make clear that the folks in Australia were paying all my expenses. I was taking my wife, Coco, with me, but her expenses were coming out of my pocket. I was not dipping into the company till to go gallivanting around.

I made the announcement to the guys who worked for us. I paid them all their money for the week of vacation and I tipped them all $50. They took their money and while I tended to things in the smoke-house, they had their little meeting in the parking lot. Maybe it comes from years of listening carefully to music, but I was able to pick up some of what they were saying. It was all negative.

"How he gon' close for a whole week and be out of town?"

"I think he done went crazy."

"We'll see what his father has to say about that."

It was unreal!

I was trying to give them a paid vacation, something my father never did, and all they could do was criticize me. I just chalked it up to folks meddling in things they couldn't control. I went ahead and got on the plane. We would be gone a week. Nothing major would happen in that short a period of time. Whatever was on people's minds could be settled when I got back.

Boy, was I wrong! My father was apparently making major moves while I was away.

My phone was ringing at 3:00 a.m. on the regular. Here I am in Australia, on the other side of the world, and the folks in Hemingway either don't know or don't care about international time differences. I'll never forget, one guy said something like, "How you gon' sleep in the middle of the afternoon with all your father's doing around here?"

When my father's preacher called, I almost lost my cool. "Your daddy doing some crazy things," he said. Just like everybody else, he concluded by saying, "Y'all need to talk."

But the reverend had been the one who tried to get us to talk even before I left town. He pulled us to the side, trying to mediate I guess. My father just said, "I ain't got nothing to talk about," and he walked off. After he woke me up in Australia I damn near hollered into the phone, "He's in your church every Sunday, why don't you mention some of this to him?" All he could say to that was, "I think y'all just need to communicate."

During this period and in the painful months afterward, there were a few people who stood by me when I needed it most. My cousin Larry "Tate" Mitchum didn't break ties with the rest of the family, but he wouldn't let them tell their lies about me stealing money and turning my back on the family without challenging what was being said. He's a little older than me, and the way he walks, he might remind you of Fred G. Sanford from *Sanford and Son*. Usually he's full of jokes and tall tales, but not when there's serious business at hand. He tried to warn me about a particular backstabbing uncle even before I realized my back was being stabbed. If I'd been paying closer attention, I would have seen it myself.

When I cooked at the pitmaster dinner in Charleston, one guy asked me, "Why does your uncle talk the way he does when your back is turned?" It seems that my uncle didn't like all the attention that was being paid to me. So every chance he got, he'd tell people, "I've been cooking hogs longer than

Rodney," or "Rodney don't really do nothing." I just took it in stride. I even asked him to come along on the Rodney in Exile tour to help cook. He never would tell me if he was going to go or not. But one monkey don't stop no show. I had so much stuff packed on my truck for that trip, I looked like Jed Clampett on *The Beverly Hillbillies*. I had a burn barrel that somebody had won at auction. I had another one that I was going to use to cook with. I had about sixty gallons of sauce, plus shovels and other tools I was going to need. By the time he came up to me and asked, "What time we leaving tomorrow?" I told him there wasn't any room for him.

Theresa Robinson and her family sell seafood on Wednesdays in my father's hometown, St. Mark. It's not far from Hemingway and I guess some of my detractors felt they could speak even more freely there. "His father needs to take that business back," they were saying, and "How's he going to take a vacation? People need to work."

"I'm hearing some things," Theresa told me one time, "and I just want you to know that if you need to talk I'm here."

My friend Terri Henning knew that a move to Charleston was a possibility. She was encouraging me to make that move and leave all the hometown/small-town foolishness behind. Joe Harvin had been a sergeant in the military, so people still call him by his rank sometimes. He's always been something of a father figure to me. "Don't just do something because you big enough to do it," he would tell me coming up. He would call me from time to time during my troubles and he still calls me to this day, "You all right? You need anything?" I appreciated all the love and support they were showing me. Yes, there were a lot of things I needed, but at that point I had no idea what they were.

The differences between a small town and a big city can be measured in square miles and population numbers. But the distances between rural America and urban America can't be calculated that easy. Because I grew up in the Hemingway-Nesmith area, I could do business with some folks on just a handshake. I could come by and settle up at the end of the week or whenever I had the money. When I took over the business, I made it a point to start paying folks on the regular and stop relying on credit like my dad did. It felt good knowing that paying on time was also buying me credit if I ever needed it again. I feel like I could call on my neighbors to help me get my crops out of the field or my truck out of the ditch more readily than I could in the big city. But I came to learn something else about the difference between city life and country life. Folks in the country are like family in good ways and bad. There are things you might do to your siblings that you'd never do to someone outside the family. You mind your manners with strangers and acquaintances. You put your guard down and put regular protocols aside with folks you know intimately. I was about to see that everybody from the bankers to the sheriff's deputies treated me like family in all the wrong ways.

The long plane rides from Sydney to Los Angeles to Atlanta to Charleston were made longer by the fact that I kept mulling over all that I was hearing about from back home. Something inside my head knew that the worst of what I was hearing was true. Something inside my heart tried to convince me that my father, despite all we had been through and all our differences, wouldn't treat me that way. I tried to negotiate some kind of agreement within myself. Setting aside our blood connection, something in my head told me that my father, who had been in business almost his entire life, wouldn't slaughter the goose that had been laying golden eggs the likes of which he had never seen before. The business was far more profitable than it had ever been before.

I'd always had the habit of saving a little bit of

what I made. But as the business grew more profitable, I found myself able to put aside a decent little nest egg. When I got to $1,700, my goal was to get that up to $2,000. Hemingway is a small town, so there's not that much to spend money on. And since I made it a point not to spend money on foolishness, my account was growing. There were a few bench marks that I remember specifically: $17,000. $26,000. $33,000. $41,000.

People talk about money being the root of all evil, but that's not true for everybody, and it wasn't true for my father. Whatever he wanted to have happen with the business while I was in Australia, it didn't revolve around more money. I think it revolved around respect and control. He wanted to be the big man in the small community. He wanted to own the small town's famous business free and clear. He wanted to call the shots.

When I got back and went to the bank, they told me I needed to talk to my father before I made a deposit. That was strange, but I figured I'd understand it all better after I talked to him. I went by the grocery store. It was open, so I could walk right in, but I noticed the locks were new. In the place where my business license used to hang, my father had a new business license.

Thinking back on it, I can see all the little signs that I had ignored in the months leading up to this. There were a lot of small things that loom large now. Going back a month earlier to December of 2015, I'd notice things the guys working around the pit would do to sabotage me. They would purposely not bring enough wood next to the burn box. So when it got time to refill it, I had to walk that extra few dozen yards to get more wood. They would leave the door to the smokehouse open, even though I'd told them the health department required it to be closed. When it came time to flip the hog, all of a sudden, everybody would disappear. Then a lot of times, they would tell on each other, like tattling kids in nursery school. One of them would tell me, "They ain't bringing the wood across the street because they don't want you to be able to get it." Then the next day a different one would say, "Man you need to keep an eye on so and so; he telling us not to bring the wood over here." Grown-ass men, acting like grown-ass assholes.

I'd been in the game too long to let some foolishness stand in my way. I'd just find somebody nearby who I knew could help flip a hog and I'd say, "You want to make $10 right quick?" So I took to keeping some cash in my pocket, and the guys who wanted to make a quick buck took to passing by and asking if I needed help.

In the months before I went to Australia, I would hear folks grumbling behind my back, saying stuff like "Rodney think he too good now." "Rodney forgot where he came from." "Rodney got too many rules." The worst one was "Rodney stealing your money." That made me laugh and get mad at the same time. How can you steal from yourself? It made no logical sense, but on another level it made all the sense in the world.

For all his toughness, my father was a soft touch when it came to loaning money. Guys would come

by with a sad story or no story at all and next thing you know my father was loaning them money that he would never see again.

The minute they found out I was in full control of the finances, they started coming at me. I got to the point that I had an answer for everything. I would be just as full of shit as they were being, but I tried to be more clever than insulting. If they said they just needed to hold some money until Thursday, I would tell them come check with me Wednesday evening.

Somebody would say, "Aw man, they about to turn my lights off!"

I'd say, "They at your house now? Then you better get over there and catch 'em."

They might say, "I need some gas money to go to the doctors." I'd tell them, "I think you need to reschedule your appointment."

If they said, "I need to borrow $20 to go get this check," I'd say, "I'll drive you and we'll go get that check together."

By then I had built a house of my own on land I owned next to the restaurant. My favorite place to sit was in a second-story room that had a clear view of the smokehouse. It was painful to see the business I had built going downhill. I would notice guys, "customers," going straight to the smokehouse and leaving with a plate of food without ever going into the store to pay. Yet my father was so focused on me and the money he apparently thought I was stealing that he didn't pay any attention to the thieves he was paying to rob him blind.

When I talk about the disadvantage of small-town familiarity, I think specifically of the way I was treated by the bank and the sheriff's deputies. I didn't know what had happened to my business license. Considering all the underhanded dealing that was taking place, I didn't want somebody to get their hands on it and use it to legitimize some business I had nothing to do with. I assumed it was still somewhere in the store and that I could just go and get it.

"I wouldn't do that if I was you," a deputy told me.

He was in his uniform when he said that to me, so I asked him if he was on the job or not? Was his statement based on some principle of law or some personal feeling? He said something like "I've known y'all since I was a young boy. Y'all need to talk this out."

What kind of legal opinion was that?

Years before all of this, I had had a joint account with my mother at another bank. We put money in the account every so often and neither of us ever took anything out. One day we realized some of our money was missing. When we brought it to the bank's attention, they pulled out some manufactured paperwork claiming we'd made withdrawals. But there were dates on their documents that we knew were false. We also knew that if we attempted any kind of legal recourse, they would invent some other paperwork to help their case. So we just decided to move all our accounts to the other bank in town.

Fast-forward: My father has opened a new business account and started making deposits in it. In addition to that, several checks had been made out to "cash" and the funds were taken from my business account. I lost about $18,000 that way. When I asked the bank for some kind of clarity, their only answer to me was "Talk to your father."

"He who angers you, controls you," I've always heard. So rather than fight the bank and have them draw up some fake paperwork like the other bank had done, I decided to let the matter rest. But it wouldn't die so easily.

I got a certified letter from my father's lawyer asking that I show up to a meeting to go over the books. Since we had gotten in trouble once before as a result of our books not being in order, I had been making sure every "i" was dotted and every "t" crossed. I wasn't stealing and I wasn't lying. I was anxious to let him see the books. I wondered why he hadn't bothered to ask to see them before.

His lawyer opened the ledger, flipped a few pages, then flipped a few more. Then he said something to my father like, "Mr. Scott, everything is accounted for." My father changed his tune and started saying stuff like, "Those are just books. They don't prove anything." Even if he didn't believe the books, he knew all the basic stuff that was happening. He knew how many hogs we were ordering each week. He knew more or less how much profit we made per pound. If he had reason to believe I wasn't taking care of the business, he had ways of proving his points.

He didn't bring up anything concrete like that. The last argument he put forward was that my mother had signed the papers agreeing to let me take over the business, not him. He had a point there, but not a good one. After his stroke, my father still suffered from paralysis. He couldn't really write his name with his left hand, so he started just making a mark. So my mother signed his name right next to his mark on the documents. Him saying that he didn't personally sign didn't change anything. The contract was still valid.

I thought that all the years I had put into the business, all the sleep I lost making it a success, and all the rebuilding I engineered after the fire and after the tax fiasco—I thought all of that would count for something.

I thought wrong.

Son to Father

My father doesn't say a whole lot. But when he wants you to know what he's thinking, he'll tell you. I wish we could have had a real conversation about why he was so opposed to the things that I was doing that he wanted to kick me out of the business and, for all intents and purposes, kick me out of the family, too. We don't speak today. The relatives and friends who chose to side with him don't speak to me either. And from my perspective, given the way they kicked me to the curb, I don't see a whole lot of reason to try to reach out.

This has put my mother in a terrible position. She and I were very close. I used to talk to her every day. She's an old-fashioned woman who believes in "love, honor, and obey" and "till death do us part." I know she loves me. I also know that, rather than take sides, she'd rather keep the peace and not rock the boat. Sometimes, my cousin will drive her the two hours from Hemingway to Charleston and she'll eat at my restaurant. Once, she surprised me and showed up on my doorstep in Charleston. Other than that, we never see each other and seldom speak. I know she doesn't like it, but it seems to suit my father just fine.

It would be easy to say that my father was afraid of change or afraid of the world outside our little part of South Carolina. But my father was in his twenties, maybe younger, when he left home for Philadelphia. He didn't just stay there a few months and leave. He made a life

in that big city, in a place that was about as different from St. Mark, South Carolina, as night is different from day. When he came home, he didn't just take a job like everybody else. He started a business. He started several of them. The problem was, despite all the land he owned, all the businesses he owned, all the crops he raised, it seemed like at the end of the day he didn't have much to show for it. As far as I could tell, there was no progress being made. There was no bank account getting fat, no fancy new house, and no profits being plowed back into the business. I think a lot of it had to do with him lending money to people who never paid it back. I think it also had to do with the fact that sometimes my father thought that working hard and working smart were the same thing.

Still, all of these things he did took courage and guts and confidence and intelligence. So I left wondering why, after all he had seen and done, he wouldn't support me doing the things I've been doing.

The best explanation I can come up with is that my father is very comfortable in the world he created. Even when folks traveled from all over the country, whether they were paupers or potentates, when they walked into Scott's Pit Cook B.B.Q., they were on his turf, eating his food by his rules. It's kind of like that sign you see in restaurants sometimes: "We reserve the right to refuse service to anyone." My father didn't refuse service to anybody that I can recall, but maybe knowing that it was his place and that he could do it made him feel in control. Even if it was his food and he took it somewhere else and served it, he wouldn't have the same control.

Most of these places and people and experiences that I've encountered in recent years have been new to me. I'm getting more and more comfortable with all of this now, but I still get a little touch of nervousness when I have to cook an important meal or cook for some big celebrity. When you're at your own restaurant cooking dozens and hundreds of hogs, you take some comfort in knowing that even if one of the hogs is not your best, you can redeem yourself with the next one. But when you're cooking one hog, one night for a bunch of strangers who have heard that you're a great pitmaster, you know you got one chance to get it right. That's a lot of pressure.

In a new situation like that it'd be good to be able to pick up the phone or sit on the porch and get some fatherly wisdom. But my father never said a whole lot to me in the past, and these days, he refuses to say anything at all.

Big City Barbecue

The first time I cooked at Blackberry Farm, the luxurious hotel and resort in the Smoky Mountains, I was still living in Hemingway and I was telling a young chef about my hometown. He asked me if I ever thought I'd leave and move to a big city. I told him, "Never." I was cooking at my family restaurant; business was good and it was improving.

Beyond the business, my material goals were to be able to travel, to have a nice place to live, and to have a nice vehicle to drive. Travel was the only one of those things that required me to leave town. It also required money. But if travel was a priority, I'd just have to save for it. I could live very happily in Hemingway for the rest of my life, I thought.

There was a pride I had in being from a place that people don't really know about. Everybody's heard of Charleston and Atlanta and New York. But only those really in the know have heard about Hemingway or Nesmith, the nearby town where I did much of my growing up. That makes us and our barbecue that much more special. People have to drive out of their way to taste Pee Dee region barbecue, and they do. The region is a part of my identity. It wasn't just a line I put in my biography, it was what I saw when I looked in the mirror.

Growing up, we didn't go to Charleston much. As exciting as it might have been to do it occasionally, it also felt good not to "need" to go there. We had what we needed where we were. It was as if we were holding our area close like a secret that only a few people knew. A lot of people probably thought I was moving up in the world when they heard I was opening a restaurant in Charleston. I felt that too, but it was a conflicted feeling. I loved Hemingway and I loved Nesmith. But my last few months in Hemingway had been painful, and a lot of that pain climbed right into my suitcase and made the drive to Charleston with me.

The source of my pain was one of the most personal relationships you can have, the relationship with a father. Here I was, at the age of forty-four, questioning whether I really knew my father. And if I was questioning that, it was a short step to an even more painful question: Did I really know myself? If my understanding of the people closest to me was so out of touch with reality, then maybe my understanding of everything else was wrong, too.

The problem with questions like these is you feel totally alone. As an only child, there was nobody I could compare notes with about my father. And my issue wasn't about fathers in general. My issue was with one father in particular: Roosevelt "Rosie" Scott. Any other insights about any other fathers would be irrelevant to my situation. Or at least that's what I thought.

The name Jim 'N Nick's was like one word to me. I didn't wonder who Jim was and it really didn't occur to me to ask. Then, I found out that Jim was Nick's father and he was the cofounder of Jim 'N Nick's. He was sixty-two years old when they opened the restaurant in 1985. I kind of assumed Nick came from some money because when I met him he owned a bunch of restaurants and knew his way around the good life in a way that only money could buy. I was wrong about that. Jim 'N Nick's struggled at first like any other small business.

When Jim 'N Nick's started to grow and succeed, it struggled another way. Nick had always wanted to have multiple restaurants, but his father was wary of Nick's plans for growth. They fought and they argued. Then Jim passed away in 2000. As difficult as that was for Nick personally, it was the lynchpin that led to the growth of the business.

Nick and his father were middle class, sophisticated white men from a big city. If they had had these kinds of troubles, maybe my situation wasn't unique. Realizing that was an important moment for me. My community in Hemingway was almost all Black. In these larger, whiter worlds that I was moving into, I had food as the connector. Food was the bridge that made it easy for me to talk to the folks I met in the FatBack Collective and the Southern Foodways Alliance and other organizations. Conversations that started about food often moved to other common interests like music and whiskey and cars. This revelation about Jim and Nick Pihakis helped me make a deeper human connection with Nick. It also helped me appreciate the things all of us have in common, whether we're sitting in the front seat of the limousine or the back, whether we used to pick tobacco or sell it.

If the death of Jim Pihakis was the event that led to the growth of Jim 'N Nick's, maybe the death of

my relationship with my father was the kick in the pants I needed for my growth and for the growth of my business. It had mattered to me that I was a good son. My father had lifted that burden off my shoulders. Now I could forget about being a good son and focus on being a good businessman.

I didn't realize this all at once. Day by day, I could feel my understanding growing and the pain of my situation decreasing. Because I had grown up working rain or shine, day or night, healthy or sick, I did what I had to do to open the restaurant in Charleston without pausing to cry about my problems. Gradually I could feel the weight lifting. I could see that there were better things behind the door that swung open than there had been behind the one that closed. I decided that my stumbling blocks would be steppingstones. Rodney Scott's Whole Hog BBQ was going to be the greatest restaurant I could make it, and my past problems weren't going to hold me back.

If I had stayed in Hemingway, it was always my plan to keep improving the business. I was going to pave the parking lot at the store, build a shed over the burn barrel and vent it better. I wanted to hire a landscaper to plant a colorful garden so that we'd have some curb appeal. People would be attracted to the flowers, then be so curious that they would come in and taste the barbecue. Now I had the freedom to make my ideas work in Charleston.

The building on King Street had been Chick's Fry House, a fried chicken place owned by Robert Stehling, who won a James Beard award at his other restaurant, Hominy Grill. We had to add barbecue pits and take out some of the deep fryers. Fortunately, when we rebuilt the pits in Hemingway we thought a lot about the best way to do it. Now we had even more ideas for making pits that would cook my kind of barbecue.

Over the years, I've found that cinder blocks are not the same as they used to be. They don't even weigh the same as they did. They're lighter. They are not as durable. They start to crumble after a few cooks. That might be fine if you're building a makeshift pit once a year for your 4th of July barbecue (I show you how to do that on page 70). They weren't so good for the four-day-per-week cooking we were

doing in Hemingway. They certainly weren't going to hold up for the everyday schedule we were planning in Charleston. So we used the mobile steel barbecue rig that I'd had built as something of a model for the pits. They would be steel like that, but would have the extra advantage of a counterweight lid so that most of the smoke would stay in the pit to provide flavor and most of the work of lifting the lid for turning the hogs would be done by the counterweight system. We also had metal doors that made it easy to shovel the coals beneath the pig.

Nick has the heart of a traditionalist and the head of a businessman. He wanted to do the barbecue the exact same way we did it in Hemingway, but he wanted to add other meats and side dishes to the menu. The criterion at first was that the new dishes needed to be something I grew up on. Then we decided that we were just looking for good food with Southern roots that would appeal to our customers. Part of Nick's concept is that a menu should be designed to guard against what he calls the veto vote. You don't want a menu that is so limited in terms of what it offers that one person in a group will veto the idea of dining at your place because there is almost nothing on the menu that fits with their diet or preferences.

Paul Yeck was crucial in terms of making the menu happen. He grew up in Oxford, Mississippi, went to culinary school in New York, and then worked for years with José Andrés, the great Spanish-born American chef. When he got ready to come back to his home region, he worked at Bottega, an Italian-focused restaurant owned by Frank Stitt, the Birmingham chef who has done so much to prove that Southern food is fine dining. Paul understood how to take the ideas and flavors I had in mind and create recipes that could be executed consistently. When you're at home you might decide not to cook a certain dish because you don't have time. In a restaurant, you can't say, "We don't have hushpuppies because the chef didn't have time to make them."

Our location was both a matter of chance—there was a vacant spot available—and a matter of choice. We are located in North-Central, a traditionally Black neighborhood known for its freedmen's cottages, small homes built for people who had just gotten out of slavery. The Rib Shack, Hank Tisdale's soul food and barbecue place, was our smoked meat predecessor on King Street back in the day. Tisdale was the father of my friend Tracey Richardson, who founded Lillie's of Charleston hot sauce company. So many of the great barbecue restaurants in this country have historically been in Black neighborhoods that I liked the idea of taking the food back to its roots. That's become something of a goal for us. When we opened in Birmingham in February of 2019, we decided to set up in Avondale, a neighborhood that used to be its own city before being incorporated into Birmingham. During segregation, much of it was a Black neighborhood. The third Rodney Scott's BBQ is in Atlanta's West End, not far from the Atlanta University Center, the Hammonds House Museum, and a lot of Afrocentric bookstores and shops.

While we were busy getting prepared to open the doors to the first Rodney Scott's BBQ in early 2017, the Charleston food community was hyping our opening day with all the enthusiasm we could have hoped for. *Eater* published a series of articles under the banner "Obsessively Track Every Moment of Rodney Scott's BBQ Opening." Then, true to the title, on January 3, 2017, Erin Perkins wrote, "Smells of Porky Goodness Almost Here at Rodney Scott's BBQ." Then, "Inspections Might Delay Rodney Scott's BBQ Opening," on February 6, and the very next day, "Take a Spin Around Rodney Scott's BBQ Before the Opening."

We sent out a press release detailing the plan for our soft opening.

Today will be a training day, and guests can come from 12 to around 3 (until food runs out) and eat for free with a suggested donation to Charleston School for Math & Science for the children in need of fun. Guests will draw from a hat for what entrée they can get, which will be either BBQ or catfish (trading in line is okay). One entrée per person, eat in or take out. Tea and Coke will be free but no alcohol.

On the day we actually opened, the line was down the block. We were slammed. One guy who was working just took his apron off and threw it against the wall. He couldn't handle the volume. My adrenaline was pumping just trying to keep up. But there were also folks wanting to come up and say hello. I couldn't rush my conversations, but I also couldn't stop work for too long. The biggest surprise during those first few days was the number of ribs we sold. We focus on whole hog barbecue and naturally we assumed that most people we would want to try our pork sandwiches. But to a lot of people, barbecue still means ribs.

Hanna Raskin, the critic for the Charleston *Post and Courier*, really captured the feeling in those first few days in the review she wrote two months later, on April 19:

For weeks before Rodney Scott's BBQ opened on upper King Street—weeks that felt like centuries to the Hemingway pitmaster's many Charleston fans—neighbors could smell that the restaurant was coming. Test runs on shiny new cookers perfumed the air for blocks with the familiar scent of smoke and the fatty notes of animal flesh. And when Food Lion shoppers and students leaving school weren't surrounded by that aroma, they could hear that Scott was working. Beyond the sizzle of ribs and chop of the cleaver, there was Scott's music, which is a constant whenever he's in a pithouse.

She ended the article by writing:

But it mostly has to do with the atmosphere that Scott has cultivated: Rodney Scott's BBQ is a remarkably happy place where people of different ages, classes, races, and sauce preferences really do share a table that runs down the middle of the glassed-in dining room.

The one crucial feature that didn't get highlighted in most of the early articles was a trademark of mine, the disco ball. I've always had a fascination with disco balls, because they just seem to take you away from the current things in life and transport you somewhere better for a minute. I know there are people who eat in our restaurants who have to get back to work in an hour or who have to rush home and bring food to the kids, but I like to think that, while they are waiting for their food, they can look up at that mirrored ball and think of good times past and even better times to come.

For the first few weeks, everybody wanted to try the new place. Fortunately, things quieted down and got to a volume level that was busy, but manageable. That allowed us some time to rethink the menu and remove a couple of items. The pork and grits just didn't sell well. With the perloo, we loved the idea of taking a Carolina Low Country rice dish and featuring it on the menu. The problem was consistency. One day it would be just right, another day it would be overcooked or undercooked.

We'd been open nearly a year when I got a text that would throw us back into extreme busy mode. In the text, John T. was congratulating me on being a semifinalist for the James Beard Best Chef Southeast award. I don't know how I got nominated. I didn't know who did the nominating and I didn't know what to expect. Then Nick called. He didn't know much more than I did. He was as surprised as I was.

The one person I knew who might have a clue about this was Sam Jones. We had both made the semifinalists list for our own restaurants after cooking for years in the family business. Sam had gotten a James Beard America's Classics award a couple of years before for Skylight Inn, his barbecue spot in Ayden, North Carolina. That award specifically honors locally owned restaurants, not chefs per se, that are loved in their communities and exemplify American cooking. Skylight Inn was established in 1947, so they had earned their stripes. But Sam had only opened his own place, Sam Jones BBQ three years ago. Rodney Scott's had only been open for a year.

People who follow those things closely might not have been shocked that two barbecue guys were nominated in one year. Aaron Franklin, the barbecue brisket master from Austin, had won the award from his region in 2015. But Sam and I were as surprised as two men could be. Chefs at expensive restaurants view a James Beard award as a goal to strive for. That's not something that was on our radar. We were just trying to serve good food.

Honor or not, being nominated kind of made us paranoid. Why did that guy order so much food for just two people? Is he a food critic? Is he a judge? Is that woman taking notes on our food or just jotting things down on her to-do list? A few weeks later we found out that we'd made it to the finalists round, and we were even more on edge.

The buzz around the award had resulted in a spike in business. When things got real busy, we didn't have enough seats. One day in particular, I remember people standing in the restaurant with food trays in their hands, but no place to sit down. We added a few more seats as well as a picnic table on the out-side. We also spruced up the landscaping with some flowers to give us a little more curb appeal.

It would have been simple to fly up to Chicago for the awards ceremony straight from Charleston. But things with Nick are never simple. Nick has two wine-maker friends in the Central Coast of California—Frank Ostini from Hitching Post, and Jim Clendenen from Au Bon Climate. For years Nick has auctioned off pig picking parties to support a charity they are involved with, so a few days before the James Beard Awards I found myself with Nick, Nicholas, and Paul in California cooking a pig. Since Hitching Post is also a steak house, we had to stop there for a meal.

Some people shouldn't be allowed to have access to private planes. One of those people is named Nick Pihakis. We were flying from California to Chicago for the awards, or so I thought. Chef Paul was in the cock-pit with Oscar, the pilot. He asked him what city he was looking at on the ground on the right. Oscar told him, Las Vegas. Paul came to the back of the plane and told Nick where we were. "Tell him to make a hard right!" Nick said. Next thing you know, I'm in Vegas.

We spent an hour or two in Vegas losing some money, then we hopped back on the plane. We got in the air and after a while Nick said, "You want some barbecue?" I said, "Why not?" So he sent a message up to Oscar. Somebody made a phone call to be sure they were open, and then we landed in Kansas City so we could go to Arthur Bryant's. Of course Nick ordered the whole damn menu.

That was a place where I was certain no one knew me. But this couple came up and congratulated me on my nomination. News travels far and fast among barbecue people. Months later, that couple was in South Carolina and ate at the restaurant.

As soon as we knew we were going to the awards ceremony, Nick had called Billy Reid, his fashion designer friend and told him we needed some tux-edos. Billy is a Southern designer who rocks the fashion world from his headquarters in Florence, Alabama. His made-to-measure specialist, Mila Pielaet, took our final measurements in the hotel room in Chicago. That was a trip! She was asking questions like, "Do you wear a watch?" and checking to see if one shoulder slumped more than the other or if one leg was bigger than the other. It was great, but still I had already gotten my shirt, socks, and tie from my man Chip Bracalente at C. Anthony's Menswear, my local clothier in Sumter. (Never forget the home team!)

All the guys were clowning and joking, but I was too nervous for that. Coco flew up to meet me at the ceremony in Chicago. We ended up getting a burger and a chicken sandwich from Shake Shack and having a quiet pre-ceremony dinner in our hotel room. I needed the downtime. Paul had been to the James Beard awards before when he worked with José Andrés. Nick and Nicholas had been to more of these big, fancy events than I had, so they weren't phased. Also, as much as I emphasize that we are a team, only one name had been nominated and only one name would be called if we won. The closer we got to the ceremony, the less I was in the mood for the usual laughing, joking, and drinking.

When I asked Paul about the day of the event, he remembers that "we" felt confident that I would win. I don't know who he meant by "we," because I wasn't confident at all. I was happy to have gotten that far and I was anxious for them to announce the winner so I could congratulate the person and get on to the relaxation part of the evening. At the awards ceremony, I felt like I needed a drink, but somehow I didn't really want one. I think Nicholas had a flask and when it came time to announce my category, I took a swig. When they announced the winner, all I can remember hearing is the "r" in my name. It was like I went deaf all of a sudden. My team all jumped out of their seats for joy. I kept my seat and looked down at my shoes. They reminded me that I had to get up and give a speech. I started walking down the aisle and it was one of the longest walks I've ever taken. I was thanking people I know along the way. There was a guy I hadn't seen in years. I stopped for a second and spoke to him. I remember telling him, "I think I have somewhere to be." Then I resumed that long walk.

Maneet Chauhan and Hugh Acheson presented the award to me. I think I only saw about four of five faces in the crowd. It was just so surreal. The first thing I said was something like "Hello y'all," or "How y'all doing?" I thanked my wife. I thanked John T. I thanked Nick Pihakis, Paul Yeck, and Nicholas Pihakis. I wanted to make sure that those names were heard from that microphone. Though "Rodney Scott's" may be one name, it stands for a whole team of people. Then I ended my speech with the words I live by: "Every day's a good day and today's a *really* good day for Rodney Scott."

After the Beard awards there's a big reception where the winners from the previous year each cook a dish. When you're walking around with a winner's medallion hanging around your neck, people come up to offer congratulations. One person said something I'll never forget: "You sit here and you think that you've only been open a year. But Mr. Scott what you need to realize is you've been cooking hogs for thirty years. You may have won for one year of Rodney Scott's BBQ, but you did it with Scott's BBQ for thirty years."

I imagined what it might have been like to win a James Beard award with my family. It would have felt good to bring that medallion back to the town where I grew up. But getting off the plane in Charleston, I wasn't thinking about the two-hour drive to Hemingway. I was thinking that I had already landed in the place I was proud to call home.

I was thinking my heart and my feet were in the same place for the first time since I left Hemingway.

Smoke on the Road

Barbecue is the most universal language of food, and even though I don't speak any language but English, I've been able to use my food to communicate with people all over the world.

People in different countries do it very differently. Some of the things people call "barbecue" we might call "grilling" in the South. But meat, wood, fire, and seasoning are universal. Barbecue is a universal language because it's the food people eat when they are celebrating. I wasn't there, but I bet the cave men would barbecue when the hunt was successful. In more recent times people would barbecue when times are good enough for them to slaughter an animal rather than keep it around to breed. Barbecue also means leisure. You can't barbecue unless you have time to relax into it. If you're in a hurry to get dinner on the table after a long day's work, you're not going to sit around a pit for hours and hours.

If you break barbecue down into its component parts—meat, wood, pit, seasoning—it's very interesting to see how things vary from place to place. The hog I cooked in Flers in France was like the hogs we used to cook in 1979 or the early 1980s. Those hogs were raised on small farms by people who cared for the animals well. That Flers pig took me back to childhood. It smelled more finished when it first started cooking than a lot of commercial American hogs do when they're almost done.

How I got to Flers is an interesting story. Hélène Dujardin, a food photographer from France, has been living in Charleston since 1997. In 2013, she and her husband, William, flew to France for her brother's funeral. That's when her cousin, who works for the city of Flers, told them about Place Charleston, a spot in Flers dedicated to the memory of the help Charlestonians gave the city after World War II. There's a plaque in downtown Charleston that explains it better than I can:

You are facing the direction of Flers de l'Orne, Normandy, France. This town inspired Charleston resident William Montgomery Bennett to initiate efforts to relieve hardships endured in Europe after World War II. The grassroots relief campaign he sparked became known as the "Medway Plan," named for the local Medway Plantation where it was organized.

With Bennett's encouragement, Charlestonians collected over 120 tons of materials for Flers. The aid, loaded onto a special transport ship christened the "Charleston Bounty," departed from

Charleston harbor on the morning of the 17th of March 1948 to alleviate the persistent hardships endured by a devastated people.

Bennett's "Medway Plan" eventually resulted in the direct assistance of hundreds of thousands of Europeans, enriching the lives of countless others in the process. The Charleston-Flers friendship became a model duplicated over three hundred times between towns in the United States and Europe. It is a friendship that continues to this day.

Charleston sent a cultural exchange delegation in 2014. Four years later, they went back, and this time they brought me along to cook a hog. I asked them what kind of hog it was. The breed is called Piétrain Landrace. It's named after the village of Piétrain in Belgium where it originated. In Normandy, they just call it a pink pig and it's very popular because it's easy to breed. The one I cooked weighed about 140 pounds. The farm where it was raised, Ferme de la Berouette, is certified organic. They raised it outside on a rotation pasture, so the pigs move to different areas of the farm eating mostly grass, some grains, and one other thing that probably makes all the difference. They eat *drêches*, the remains of the grains that are used to make beer. I don't know if the *drêches* have any alcohol in them. For the pigs' sake, I hope they do.

I cooked the pink pig over oak in France and it cooked just like the oak at home. The problem came when I got ready to make the sauce with vinegar. It was so strong that I had to do some serious diluting to get it right, but eventually I did.

After a hog has been on the pit a couple of hours, I can smell whether it's a good hog. I've cooked a few times in the Bay Area at 4505 Burgers & Barbecue Restaurant. They would get hogs from Rancho Llano Seco, a cross of Duroc, Yorkshire, and Landrace breeds. Long before the meat hits my tongue, I know these are not your average pigs.

Traveling the world, I've gotten to see a lot of different approaches to cooking something that I've been cooking all my life. I remember as a kid seeing Australia on a globe and wondering what it was like so far away. My romance with the country goes back that far. So when Morgan McGlone, a New Zealander who used to be Sean Brock's chef de cuisine at Husk and who now lives in Australia, invited me to cook Down Under, it was a dream come true. It's funny, though, because when they first asked me to cook in Melbourne, I said yes without thinking. I assumed they meant Melbourne, Florida. I figured it would be a long drive, but me and my truck like to hit the road. Then I thought for a minute and checked back with them. That's when I realized which Melbourne they were talking about.

In Australia, we cooked with a wood they call river red gum. The center of it is a beautiful reddish orange. People use it for furniture, because it's so pretty. The tree itself is incredible, too; it can live more than 500 years and can grow to be 150 feet tall. It smells and burns like oak. The first time I went, we constructed a pit using cinder blocks and rebar. The next time I went, a guy fabricated me a pit out of metal. It turned out to be the wrong kind of metal. It melted and we had to improvise another pit.

The FatBack Collective has a lot of friends including Anya Fernald, the CEO of Belcampo Meat Co, the Oakland-based group of restaurants and meat markets. She was helping to promote ecotourism resorts in Uruguay and Belize, and Nick got the bright idea of having the FatBack Collective visit those places and cook with the local ingredients. In Uruguay, I say that we cooked the Three Little Pigs because instead of one big hog we were given three suckling pigs. Nick and Pat Martin were my partners on barbecued pork duty. Other chefs on the trip roasted vegetables and some braised meat. I had never cooked on a totally open pit before. Even in the early days in Hemingway, when we didn't have metal covers for the pits, we'd put sheet metal or boards over the hogs to keep more of the smoke in. Drew Robinson, who was a chef at Jim 'N Nick's at the time, wrote a journal about the trip that was published online by Food Republic. Thanks to Drew's article, I can tell you what the menu was: deviled eggs, boudin, fried squash blossoms stuffed with goat cheese, smothered chicken, barbecue pork, arugula salad with fava beans and strawberries, broccoli leaf coleslaw, meaty beans, olive oil-braised beans, coal-roasted beets, and cast-iron peach cobbler baked in the coals à la Angie Mosier.

When we cooked in Belize, some of the guys went out to the forest to get some wild hearts of palm while the rest of us cooked the pig over a spit. You see meat being roasted so often in old Western movies that you think it's easy to cook like that, but it's not. That thing has to constantly be turning or the skin will be crispy before the meat is cooked. Fortunately, we had an electric spit turner doing the work. In the old days, turning the spit used to be someone's job. (I'm glad those days are over!) We stuffed the pig with some seasonings and that turned out to be some good eating! It came out kind of like porchetta—crispy on the outside and beautifully tender and garlic-scented on the inside.

All things aside, most of my cooking has been focused on trying to get one dish right—our style of barbecued pork. Sometimes I wish I'd started on my travel journey earlier, but then again, the reason people invite me to these places to cook is that I spent all that time in Hemingway perfecting our barbecue to the standard of people who have been eating versions of Pee Dee barbecue for decades before I was born. In essence, my customers in Hemingway taught me to cook for the world.

BARB

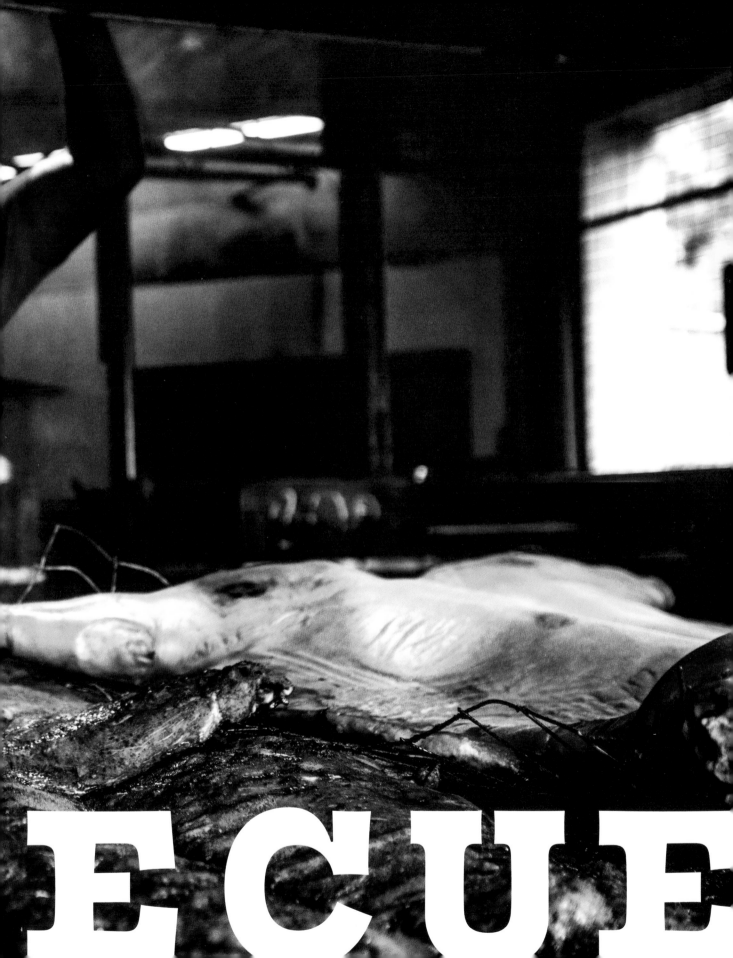

E CUE

My Style of Cooking

Even when I tell people I cook barbecue and I'm from South Carolina, they don't know exactly what to expect. If you want to understand the confusion, just look up a map of South Carolina barbecue sauces. You'll see that the regions are divided by sauces. Some are mustard-based, some have a lot of ketchup, some have a little ketchup with vinegar and peppers, and some are like mine, mostly vinegar and pepper. I would try to tell you what cities and counties do it this way or that, but it wouldn't do you much good. The border lines between sauces are not straight, and everywhere you go there's somebody doing it a little different than the local norm. One constant in South Carolina is that everywhere you go in this state, pork is king. You can find beef and chicken on some menus, but they usually aren't the main attraction.

When I barbecue, the coals are placed directly under the meat. The fat from the meat drips down directly onto the coals. The smell of the smoke immediately changes once that fat hits the burning coals. The aromas from the smoke off of those wood coals and the smoke off that simmering fat creates a magical combination of the flavors. I think that's the secret to the taste of my barbecue.

Of course, cooking like that has its dangers: Fat + Heat = Fire. When you allow the fat to drip this way, you increase the likelihood of a pit fire. You can avoid small occasional flare-ups if you use all your senses.

* Consistently check your thermometer to see if your temperature is getting too hot. Place your hand on the wood or sheet metal you have covering the pit. Get used

to how it feels when it is burning hot or when the temperature has dropped.

* Look at the color and volume of smoke coming out of the pit. When the meat is smoking, the smoke is a white-gray color and it floats out of the pit. When you have a flare-up in the pit, you'll start to see the smoke darken and increase in volume.

* Learn to listen for the rhythm of the fat dripping from the hog. When it's cooking properly, you should expect to hear the sizzle of fat dripping every 4 to 6 seconds. If it's coming down faster than that, it's cooking too quickly and has probably flared up.

* Your nose is important, too, but it takes a little longer to develop.

After years of experience, I have learned to cook without a thermometer. But we have thermometers in all the pits at the restaurants so that cooks with less experience can keep track of the cooking process. When I hear the fat dripping in that 4- to 6-second range, I can almost guarantee that if I look at the thermometer it will be in the 225° to 250°F sweet spot that I like to cook in.

Once, we had been cooking all night in advance of a tailgate for the Iron Bowl. For those of you who are not from Alabama, the Iron Bowl is the annual football game between Auburn University and the University of Alabama. To hear folks from Alabama tell it, the Iron Bowl is kind of like the Super Bowl, only more historic and more intense. That's because these two teams have been playing each other ever since the first football season after Adam and Eve left the Garden of Eden. It's that serious.

We had gotten a late start putting the hog on the pit. Not long after we flipped the hog, it was time to load the rig and drive across town to the tailgate party. We were thinking that the pit was still hot, but it was not going to flare up. We thought we were safe. As we were driving, I was seeing black smoke coming out of the pit. By the time we were able to pull to the side of the road, the hog was on fire and we were scrambling to pour sauce into the pit to put the flames out. We were able to save about half of the meat. Anybody who showed up late to the party probably didn't get any pork.

Lesson learned. Always know how hot your pit is.

The smoke is my primary seasoning. But I add our dry seasoning blend as well as our vinegar-based sauce while the meat is still on the pit. During the last few minutes on the heat the sauce cooks into the meat. I think you get a flavor that way that you don't get from simply adding sauce at the table. We are careful not to over-sauce the meat. There is extra sauce available so that folks can add more if they wish.

Wood

When it comes to wood, I believe that it's not so much what kind you use as how you use it. The wood is responsible for imparting a lot of the flavor to your barbecue. But as long as you are using hardwoods, like oak, pecan, and hickory, your meat should have a good taste. You need trees that don't have sap in them. (No pine trees!) The first thing that influences the choice of woods is what you have available. I don't think there's any mesquite in South Carolina, so that's not what I use.

The barbecue-wood trees we have the most of in my part of South Carolina are oak, pecan, and hickory. Oak is my favorite. I love the flavor it gives to the meat and I like the way it burns. Pecan has a nice mild aroma. It's a quick heat. It burns very fast. It's hard to maintain an all-night cook with just pecan. Hickory will stay hot longer than pecan without burning out. But it has such strong flavor that it can be overpowering. The mix I prefer is 50 percent oak, 30 percent pecan, and 20 percent hickory. Wood that has been recently chopped and has not been given a chance to dry out is called green wood. That has nothing to do with its color. I prefer a mix of old and green wood. Because green wood has a higher moisture content, it will burn more slowly and last longer. Old wood is dryer so it's easier to light quickly. But it also burns quickly. If you find yourself with all old wood, you'll be refilling the burn barrel more often. My ideal mix of the two is 60 percent green wood and 40 percent old.

Don't worry too much if you don't have that mix. The green versus old woods will have more impact on the cooking than on the flavor of the meat.

When I cook in different parts of the country, people will often have different kinds of wood for me to try. I've cooked with some fruitwoods before—apple, peach, and cherry. I've always used them like flavor enhancers. They might have been like 20 percent of the wood I was using. It was a nice change of pace, but I guess I'm kind of a creature of habit. Give me my oak, pecan, and hickory and that'll be that.

These days, when you go to the supermarket, there's often a bundle of fireplace wood for sale. I'd be wary of that. First of all, you have to be sure it's hardwood. Look for the bark. If the bark has been trimmed off, don't buy it.

I usually keep a bag of hardwood lump charcoal around, especially if I'm doing events out of town. If I get behind in my cook and need some coals immediately, I can go to the bag of charcoal and not have to wait for the burn barrel to deliver.

If you're using an offset smoker like they do in Texas and Oklahoma, you can feed pieces of wood straight into the burn barrel (see page 76). If you are using a more traditional barbecue pit, like a Weber or a 55-gallon drum, your best bet is probably to use hardwood lump charcoal (which is just wood burned down to coal). Avoid charcoal briquettes, which contain a lot of binders and fillers. Lump charcoal burns hotter and faster, which means you might have to add coals to the pit more often. But it's worth the trouble. Lump charcoal is different from the coals that we scoop out from the burn barrel and use for our barbecue. I learned that the one time I made charcoal back in 2016.

I decided to do it just to see what it was all about. I'll never do that again! It's a lot of trouble and not worth it to me given all the quality hardwood charcoal on the market these days. I do not intend to ever make my own charcoal again, but if you want an idea of how it's done, here it is: First you need a closed container or space because the wood needs to smolder in an airless environment. You can use a 55-gallon drum that can be tightly sealed. Fill the barrel about halfway with hardwood pieces and set them on fire. When you have a good flame going, add enough wood to come to the top of the barrel, but not so much that you can't close the barrel. Once that wood is flaming, put the top back on the barrel and close it tightly. Let it burn sealed like that for several hours or optimally overnight. After the barrel is cool, open it up. What you'll have inside is charcoal.

Building the Pit

Building a pit is a commitment. Between the shopping for materials and the actual construction of the pit, you're talking a few hours. And that's before you spend the twelve hours cooking the hog. Needless to say, I think it's worth it. And once you build your first pit and cook your first hog, you will, too. On one hand the pit is a necessary piece of equipment. You can't really cook a whole hog without one. On the other hand, it's much more than that. The pit becomes the centerpiece for a gathering. If it's a little cold outside, people congregate around the pit for the warmth and fellowship. Even if it's not cold, I think we all have a little fascination with fire. The idea of controlling and using something that can be so powerful and so destructive is almost like a drug. Even looking at how the embers still glow long after you pull the pig off is kind of beautiful.

Building a pit is also not that hard. Once you have everything you need, it's really a matter of assembling it. You just put one block on top of the other. Still, it might make sense to build the pit one day ahead and cook your hog the next. That way you can focus on one thing at a time.

62 (8 × 8 × 16-inch) cinder blocks

7 (48-inch) lengths of rebar

2 pieces of 14-gauge plain welded wire mesh cut into 64-inch lengths (do not use coated wire) *

Sheet metal or plywood large enough to cover the pit

Grill thermometer with probe

Electric drill

Angle grinder

Shovel

Safety goggles

Hammer

Pavers, optional * *

* *Chicken wire is too thin to support the weight of the hog when you are flipping it. If you must use chicken wire, you should double or triple it for extra support.*

** *If you are building it on your lawn or on a piece of ground you want to protect, paving stones placed on the floor of the pit could minimize the damage, though there is no guarantee that the grass will survive.*

(instructions continue)

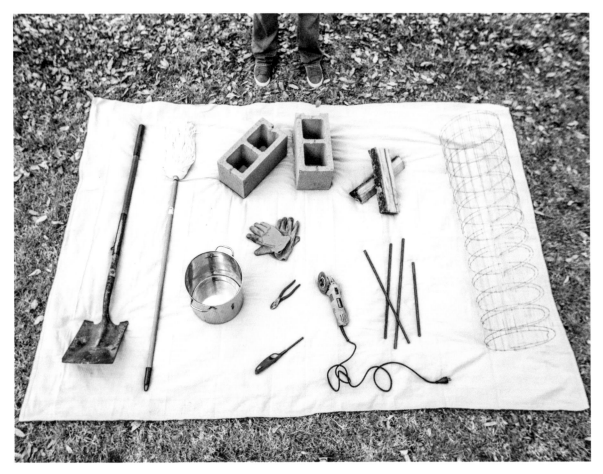

First lay down the width of the pit. Take 3 cinder blocks and place them end-to-end lengthwise to a length of 48 inches. Take a fourth cinder block and turn it so that it meets the last block at a 90-degree angle and begins the lengthwise wall. The total width of the pit will be 56 inches, or 3½ blocks.

Continue along the lengthwise wall placing 4 more blocks end-to-end. Place a fifth block at a right angle so that the total length of the pit will be 88 inches or 5½ blocks.

Lay the blocks for the second width wall just as you did for the first. Starting with the block that was laid at a 90-degree angle to the length wall, lay 3 more blocks end-to-end until the wall is 54 inches or 3½ blocks. Then lay the second length wall just as you did the first.

Now build the second layer of the wall. Place the blocks on top of the first ones, making sure to stagger the cinder blocks so that each block rests astride the 2 blocks below it. When you lay the second width wall, leave out one cinder block one row from the bottom. That will be the hole through which you can shovel coals into the pit.

Once the pit is three cinder blocks high, it's time to insert the bars of rebar that will hold the pig. The bars should be placed crosswise and 7 inches apart.

If you have a drill or angle grinder handy, put on safety goggles and notch out roughly ½-inch-deep notches in the cinder blocks on the long side of the pit for the bars large enough to accommodate the rebar. Use a hammer to knock out the notches. Then place the fourth and final layer of cinder blocks on top. (If you can't cut the holes, don't worry. Your cinder blocks won't sit flush, but the pit will still be stable.)

Place one piece of the welded wire mesh on top of the rebar (see following page). Set the other one aside until it is time to flip the hog.

Drill a hole in the sheet metal or plywood you will be using to cover the pit. The hole should be big enough to accommodate the thermometer.

Building a Burn Barrel

If you only plan on cooking a whole hog once or twice a year, you might want to save yourself the trouble of making a burn barrel. The advantage of a burn barrel is that you can feed large pieces of wood in the top, and the embers you need for cooking will automatically fall down to the bottom. You can easily scoop them up from there to put under your hog. In the old days, we stacked wood on a patch of ground using larger logs to form a teepee shape, then we shoveled the hot coals from the bottom of the pile of embers. That method works, but there are some problems with it. Long before the pig is finished cooking, the logs you've used to frame your fire will burn and need to be replaced. You also have to worry about the occasional spark flying and landing on something flammable. And, of course, you need to find a patch of ground that is not near anything too flammable.

One time I was invited to cook out of town and they didn't have a burn barrel. I used a large cast-iron fire pit, the kind people sometimes use like a campfire to gather around on chilly nights when they want to sit outside. You can buy fire pits for less than $100, although I've seen them for several hundred dollars as well. If you go the fire pit route, be sure you buy one that has a wide enough circumference to allow you to easily dip your shovel beneath the burning wood to reach the coals.

Building a burn barrel will definitely make your life easier in the long run if you use it often. Turn the page to see what you need and how to do it.

55-gallon steel drum (if you don't have easy access to a clean used one, buy one online)

Protective goggles

Long sleeves and pants (to protect you from sparks and shards of metal flying as you make your cuts)

Angle grinder with a cutting wheel attached (and a grinding wheel if you want to smooth your cuts)

Hand drill with metal hole saw attachment

3 (28-inch) lengths of rebar

1 (32-inch) length of rebar

6 (8 × 8 × 16-inch) cinder blocks

Measure the width of the blade of the shovel that you will be using to feed the coals into the pit. With the gallon drum standing up, use chalk or a permanent marker to trace a hole at the bottom of the barrel, big enough for the shovel to go in with at least an inch clearance on all sides.

Turn the barrel* on its side. Use the angle grinder with the attached cutting wheel to cut out the hole that you marked for the shovel. If you want to smooth the rough edges of your cuts, you can attach a grinding wheel to the angle grinder and make the edges smooth.

The burn barrel in the photos, which is an old burn barrel, has had the bottom cut off of it. These days, I prefer to leave the bottom of the barrel intact, because it's more stable that way.

Now use your angle grinder to cut a hole near the top of the barrel, roughly the same size as the hole you cut at the bottom to put your shovel through. This is the opening you will use to feed the wood into. Finally, cut a 6- to 8-inch hole in the top, roughly in the center, to act as a chimney. That minimizes the amount of sparks from the burning wood that fly out. To cut the small hole, use a metal hole saw attached to a hand drill.

You'll need to insert some rebar into the drum to keep the bigger pieces of wood suspended above the coals. That way it's easy to shovel out only the small coals and place them in the pit. The "rolling hoops" (the protruding rings around a drum) divide the drum into three sections. Just above the lower rolling hoop (the one nearer to the bottom), drill 3 holes about 6 inches apart. Drill 3 holes directly across from these. Insert the three 28-inch lengths of rebar through those holes from one side of the barrel to the other.

Rotate the drum 90 degrees from the holes you just drilled and drill a hole an inch or two higher than the 6 holes you just drilled. Then drill a matching hole on the direct opposite side of the barrel. Insert the 32-inch length of rebar. It will be perpendicular to the 3 bars you just inserted. In addition to helping to hold the large pieces of wood, that bar can also serve as your handle when you need to move the burn barrel.

Place the 6 cinder blocks on their sides (edge to edge) to create a platform. Place the burn barrel on the platform.

Starting the Fire

Wood (such as oak, pecan, hickory, mesquite, or any other hardwood; see page 68)

1 or 2 cardboard boxes torn into several pieces, sprinkled liberally with vegetable oil and/or bacon grease

Place 5 or 6 pieces of wood through the hole near the top of the barrel, letting them drop down to the rebar below.

Stuff the pieces of cardboard into the bottom hole, under the bars. Set them on fire. Gradually, that fire should catch the wood above it. Allow that to burn until all of the wood in the barrel is burning, about 30 minutes. Then add a few more pieces of wood through the top hole. You do not want a raging fire, just a steady blaze. It will take 45 minutes to 1 hour for the fire to produce enough coals to start cooking the hog.

You'll know that you are ready to start cooking when there are enough coals at the bottom to fill at least 4 shovelfuls and preferably more.

Cooking the Hog

WHAT'S the first thing that comes to your mind when you think of an epic feast? I bet it's a roasted pig with an apple in its mouth. That says "feast" in ways that a Thanksgiving turkey or standing rib roast doesn't quite say it. Maybe it's because the word "hog" symbolizes gluttony and greed, so to feast on a hog is the height of feasting.

Whole hog is king in the barbecue world. Barbecuing briskets and pork shoulders well is an art that takes time, skill, and dedication. But it doesn't take the twelve hours of concentration that a whole hog requires.

When you cook hogs day in and day out like I do, you can lose sight of this. We might cook a whole hog, but we serve it pound by pound. For our day-to-day customers, the pork is a sandwich, not a feast. But when I think back on our business in Hemingway, and how people would be rushing to get their orders in for a hog to serve on Thanksgiving or Christmas, I remember how special this delicacy is. I think about the old days when people raised their own hogs. Slaughtering one of those animals took a lot more effort and emotion than it does to call the butcher and order some meat. I try to remember that, especially when I'm cooking for an important event. And you should keep that in mind, too. This is a serious undertaking, but it's also rewarding.

Get a fresh, never frozen, hog. Before buying it, examine the hog for any obvious signs of bruising, broken bones, or other indications that it is not a good hog. Ask the butcher to crack the spine but not cut it all the way through. That way you can butterfly the hog, without separating it into two pieces. Be sure that the skin is not punctured or the melting fat will run off into the pit and cause a fire. I like to have the head and feet removed so that the hog fits more easily on the pit.

Burn barrel (see page 76)

½ cord * hardwood, such as oak, pecan, or hickory

2 pieces of 64-inch-long 14-gauge plain welded wire mesh * * (do not use coated wire)

1 whole hog (120 to 140 pounds), dressed (organs and inedible parts removed)

1 large long-handled shovel

1 large piece of sheet metal or plywood to cover the pit

Grill thermometer

1 gallon distilled white vinegar, for dousing the flames

2 pairs heat-resistant gloves

1 long-handled metal cooking spoon

1 gallon Rodney's Sauce (page 211) in a large bucket

1 clean rayon mop * * *

Sauces, for serving

Set up the burn barrel as directed on page 76. Once enough coals have dropped to fill the shovel 4 times, you are ready to start cooking.

Place one piece of the welded wire mesh in the pit over the rebar. I prefer to put the hog on a cold pit. It is easier to maneuver around a cold pit if you need to make adjustments. Now place the butterflied hog belly-side (cut-side) down on the welded wire.

Take a full shovel of coals and, using the hole in the pit where one cinder block has been removed, insert a shovelful and spread them under the shoulders of the hog.

(instructions continue)

* *A cord is about the amount of wood it would take to fill half the bed of a 6-foot pickup truck.*

* * *Chicken wire is too thin to support the weight of the hog when you are flipping it. If you must use chicken wire, you should double or triple it for extra support.*

* * *I prefer rayon mops to cotton mops because the cotton will start to break down once the vinegar hits it.*

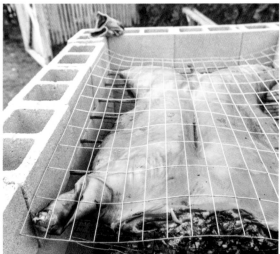

Take another full shovel of coals and do the same under the hams (hind legs). Sometimes people talk about "firing the shoulders," or "firing the hams," I don't put separate piles of coals under each shoulder or ham. I spread the coals across from shoulder to shoulder and ham to ham. Do not put coals directly under the belly and back. Those thinner parts of the hog will get cooked by heat generated by the coals under the shoulders and hams.

Cover the pit with the sheet metal or plywood and insert the thermometer through the hole you have cut in the top. After 10 to 15 minutes, fire the hog again with a full shovel of coals under the shoulders and a full shovel of coals under the hams, spreading them out like you did before. You need to get the temperature of the pit up to 250°F and maintain a steady temperature between 225° and 250°F by adding more coals whenever the temperature drops below 225°F.

In the first 4 hours of cooking, the hog is in what I call the danger zone. You need to pay close attention. If the pit falls below 200°F for any significant period of time, you're in danger of spoiling the hog. It will start to smell foul or even rancid. At that point, there is nothing you can do but throw away the hog. It cannot be salvaged. To avoid this, for the first 4 hours, check your thermometer every 10 to 15 minutes and fire the hams and shoulders with a half shovel of coals each time. If the temperature dips below 225°F, add slightly more than a half shovel of coals. If the temperature is at or above 250°F, wait an extra few minutes before adding more coals.

After 4 hours, you should be out of the danger zone, meaning your hog has reached a high enough internal temperature that you are not in danger of it spoiling. If at any time you have flames flare up in the pit, douse them with the vinegar.

Once you've done this a few times, you can start to rely on your other senses to tell you what's happening in the pit. You can hear if the hog is cooking too fast by how often the fat drips down onto the coals. (It should happen every 4 to 6 seconds.)

Depending on the size of the hog and the heat of the pit, it can take anywhere from a total of 10 to 12 hours for the hog to be completely cooked. I have a few techniques I use to determine that a hog is ready. If you press on the shoulders or hams, you should be able to feel a separation where the meat has separated from the skin at the thickest parts. There are also small bones that

are part of the bone structure of both the hams and the shoulders. Those bones should be visible at each of the places where the feet had been removed. If you can pull that bone out, then you know the hog is done. Finally if you insert a thermometer into the thickest part of the ham or shoulder, you should get a temperature reading of about 185°F.

Now you're ready to flip the hog and crisp the skin. This seems obvious and easy, but I've seen enough disasters and been a part of enough disasters to know that you can't take flipping the hog for granted. It's one of the last things you will do in cooking the hog, and if you get it wrong it could mean that all that other work is wasted.

Put the second piece of welded wire mesh on top of the hog. Post one person at the front of the hog, with the shoulders and another person at the back with the hams. Be sure to discuss in which direction you will turn the hog. Do a dry run before you flip the hog. Have one person count off "1-2-3-flip." Using heat-resistant gloves, hold the top and bottom wires together in a tight grip. Lift and turn the hog and gently place it back down on the pit so that it is skin-side down.

(instructions continue)

To crisp the skin, spread 2 full shovels of coal at the front of the hog and 2 at the back for a total of 4 shovels full of coals. This time spread the coals not just under the hams and shoulders, but under the entire hog. Take your cooking spoon and loosen up the meat around the bones in various parts of the hog, especially at the hams and shoulders, but also at the backbone and ribs.

Place the bucket of Rodney's sauce and the mop next to the pit. Saturate the mop with the sauce and bounce it lightly over one of the shoulders four or five times until most of the sauce is on the meat. Dip the mop again and repeat the sauce procedure for the belly and chest areas on the same side of the hog. Dip the mop again and sauce the ham side. Then repeat the entire process on the other side of the hog. You will probably have used just about all of the sauce at this point. The sauce will be boiling in the cavity of the hog. Cover the pit again and let the hog finish over the hot coals until the meat is tender and the sauce is thoroughly cooked through, 30 minutes to 1 hour.

(instructions continue)

Remove any excess fat and any bones that easily slip out and discard them. I like to mix the meat from the various sections of the hog all together. That way the meat from the drier, thicker cuts like the loin is mixed with the meat from the moister, fattier sections like the belly. It also means you can get all the flavors and textures in one bite.

To do this, I recommend pulling all the meat to the center of the hog and mixing it thoroughly. If you prefer you can separate the various sections of the hog into individual pans and serve it separately.

Serving the meat while the hog is still on the pit can be dangerous. It is always possible that a flame will flare up while your guests are serving themselves. I recommend moving the hog from the pit before serving.

We have a "hog pan," which is a custom-made sheet metal tray that we had built so that it would fit through just about any doorway when we are cooking offsite. It is 33 × 36 inches and 6 inches deep. If you have a similar tray, or if you have a table you can serve a whole hog from, lift the hog with the bottom wire and transfer it to the tray or table. If you have a tray, it will take two people to lift the hog and two people to hold the tray. Don't try to be Superman. Have people help. It's not worth it to risk dropping the hog.

If you don't have a surface that will accommodate a whole hog, you can pull the meat while the hog is still on the pit and transfer it to serving trays. Once the meat has been put into trays, you can break up the crisped skin into pieces of cracklin' to serve alongside. Back in Hemingway, most people would eat the meat on sandwiches with nothing but a little extra sauce. For a real feast, serve with potato salad and coleslaw and all of your other favorites side dishes.

A Few Thoughts on Sandwiches

At the restaurant, our standard sandwiches were designed to highlight the barbecue. For the most part they consist of just three things—meat, toasted bun, and sauce. The Rod's Original is the exception. It's served open-faced on white bread with pork skins on top.

There are a few sandwich variations you can easily engineer using the recipes in this book. I have been known to put some baked beans on a pork sandwich. If you put some coleslaw on top of the meat, our barbecue pork sandwich will taste like it has a Memphis accent.

The smallest sandwich on the menu might also be the most special. The Ike Sandwich is a nod to my son. (His name is really Braylon, but when his grandmother saw him and his mother bickering back and forth, she started calling them Ike and Tina because of the way Ike and Tina Turner fought in the movie *What's Love Got to Do with It*. The name stuck, at least with me, and I still call him Ike most of the time.) The sandwich is really just a child's portion of the pork sandwich. When we opened, my son was seven or eight years old, and seeing his name on the menu just lit up his world. So now it's never coming off, even though he can eat more than a child's portion these days.

FROM TH

Grilling on a Traditional Grill

I've owned several barbecue grills and cooked on several more. Right now my home equipment is a Big Green Egg. I use it for grilling because it gets hot real fast, holds its temperature, and can easily adjust from high-temperature grilling to low-and-slow smoking. I've had Weber grills in the past. They're great, too. The drawback with them, I found, was that if you were cooking something for a long time, you'd have to add more charcoal from time to time. I've also used 55-gallon drum barbecue pits and similar commercial pits that are based on the 55-gallon drum design. They cook great, but be careful. They tend to rust out unless you clean them thoroughly. People tend to assume that once they take the food off the grill, the work is done. But all that ash and bits of charcoal you leave in the bottom of the grill will retain moisture when it rains, or even when it's very humid outside. After a few months of that, you might find your grill has rust holes in it. Those holes will let in air, so even if you are able to cook on it, you won't have the amount of control over your heat that you'd like. Remember: Cleaning the grill ain't just for looking good; it's also for cooking good.

Grilling Technique

First prep your grill. Using a grill brush, clean the grate to ensure that it is free of rust, debris, or ash from any previous use.

Then you can get your fire going. There are several devices you can use to get the grill started. They range from flame thrower-like devices to electric charcoal starters to charcoal chimney starters. (I recommend that you never use lighter fluid to start your fire.)

I have a low-tech, low-cost approach that I think works just as well: Take a pizza delivery box ripped into pieces or an equivalent amount of cardboard, or take two sections of your daily newspaper with the individual pages crumpled up into several balls. Wet these with a few tablespoons of bacon grease or other cooking oil. Place it in a pile on the lower rack of the grill, the one reserved for charcoal. Stack 8 to 12 pieces of charcoal on top of that. Set the paper alight. The paper will burn into flames and light the charcoal.

For the fire, you ultimately want the charcoal to be glowing red and white, not flaming. Once the charcoals are hot, add more charcoal a few pieces at a time so as not to smother the coals. Spread the charcoal out to cover about three-quarters of the grill bottom, leaving a small area that will remain slightly cooler if you need to move items away from the hottest part of the grill.

Return the cooking grate to the grill. Crack the vents at the bottom of the grill slightly to allow air flow to feed the fire. Close the lid of the grill. Keeping the lid closed is crucial both to maintain your temperature and to keep as much smoke in the pit as possible to flavor the meat. When the lid is hot to the touch and you can hold your palm on it for no more than a few seconds, it is about ready to cook on. If the grill doesn't have a built-in thermostat, insert your thermometer to check that it is the appropriate temperature for your recipe.

One of the most difficult things about barbecuing is maintaining the proper temperature. There are three main factors to keep in mind—the wood/charcoal, the airflow, and the meat itself. The meat will drip fat into the coals and when it does it could flare up. You can hear and smell when there's a flare-up. The fat will be dripping faster because the meat is cooking quick. You'll get a smell kind of like what you get when you spill grease on the stove. If you see smoke pouring out instead of seeping out, it means you have a real fire starting. You can douse those flames with vinegar.

As to airflow, a good barbecue grill will have adjustable vents. When the vents are closed, they aren't allowing any air to get in. If you open them slightly, enough air should get in to feed the coals and maintain the temperature without causing the coals to flare up. If your temperature starts to drop, opening the vents should help.

The other factor is the amount of charcoal you have in the grill. Remember, you only want to use enough charcoal to cover about three-quarters of the grill. If the temperature of the grill starts to drop, open the vents to let more air in or lift the lid of the grill.

Most of the recipes in this section call for you to maintain a temperature between 225°F and 250°F. Once your grill has achieved that temperature, you can begin putting the meat on to cook. For those recipes that are cooked more quickly—the hamburger, pork steak, and veggies—the grill should be heated to a temperature range between 400°F and 450°F. To achieve that temperature, leave the vents of the grill open to allow more airflow.

Smoked Prime Rib

IT took ten years for me to feel confident enough to put steak back on the menu. At our place in Hemingway, I would just keep trying different techniques and cuts of meat, but none of them came out the way I wanted them to. My goal was to smoke a steak on the pit in a similar way to how we smoked our hogs. I wouldn't smoke a steak as long as I smoked a whole hog, but I'd leave it on the pit long enough to get that smoked flavor. In the end, I wanted to have a tender, juicy steak. My inspiration was a disappointing steak that I'd had at a national chain. I didn't know exactly what I wanted, but I knew what I didn't want, and it was that.

I tried marinating it. I tried using just salt and pepper. But I never could quite get it right. Part of the problem might have been that I was also trying different cuts of steak. Finally, I decided that I'd focus on one cut—rib eye. First of all, rib eye is boneless. Since I was selling the steaks on a sandwich, that was important. Second, rib eyes are more tender than New York strips and more flavorful than filet mignon. One day, I presented my mother with the sandwich I wanted to sell, a 1-inch-thick rib eye on two slices of white bread with some American cheese. By that time she'd tasted a whole bunch of my mistakes. This version she liked. It wasn't tough like some of the others, and the flavors had married well. We put it on the menu as a Saturday special.

The steaks sold, but they weren't the big hit I was hoping for. I would prepare about a dozen of them and probably sell eight on the average Saturday. People came for the pork because that's what they knew. They weren't used to buying steak from us.

At the restaurant these days, we sell the steak sliced on a sandwich, not as an à la carte item. This version uses a thick cut of steak so it can spend a couple of hours soaking up smoke flavor on the grill and still not be overcooked. I like to serve it with potatoes roasted on the grill. Use the Loaded Potatoes (page 158) and eliminate the toppings.

1¼ cups Rib Rub (page 205)

3- to 4-pound rib-eye roast

2 cups Rodney's Sauce (page 211)

Make the brine: In a medium saucepan, bring 4 cups water to a boil. Add 1 cup of the rib rub and stir until fully dissolved. Transfer the mixture to a container large enough to hold 1 gallon of water and the meat. Add the roast and 12 cups water and refrigerate for 8 hours for a 3-pound piece of meat and 10 hours for 4 pounds.

Remove the roast from the brine (discard the brine) and allow it to come to room temperature. This may take an hour or two, but it helps you get a more even cook.

Fire up your grill to 250°F (see Grilling Technique, page 95).

Pat the roast dry. Sprinkle the remaining ¼ cup rib rub on all sides of the roast. Using butcher's twine, truss the roast lengthwise so that the rib eye cap, filet, and tail are all compressed. (This step isn't necessary, but I recommend it, as it helps a boneless cut of meat cook more evenly.)

Place the roast on the grill grate, close the grill, and cook about 1 hour for a 3-pound prime rib or slightly longer for a larger one. The meat will have browned and the outside will start to look done. Mop the meat with the sauce, turn it over, and mop the other side. Close and cook until the roast reaches an internal temperature of between 120°F and 125°F for rare; between 130°F and 135°F for medium-rare; and between 140°F to 145°F for medium. This should take 2½ to 3 hours.

When the roast has reached your desired level of doneness, take it off the grill and let it rest for 15 minutes. Then carve and serve.

Mopping

To cook a whole hog my way you need a mop and a bucket. I'm sure you can figure out other ways to spread a lot of sauce on a whole hog, but that's the way we've always done it and it works. Obviously, you need to buy a new mop and a new bucket, or bucket-sized pot, and use them only for cooking. Avoid 100% cotton mops. I know they are more natural, but the vinegar in the sauce destroys them. I recommend a rayon mop head.

When I'm cooking barbecue on my smaller, backyard grill (like a Weber), I use a smaller mop. It has a 16-inch handle and it works fine. You can find mops like that in most of the places that sell barbecue equipment, or you can use a large basting brush.

Rodney's Spare Ribs

SERVES 6

IN this recipe I'm talking strictly about pork spare ribs with the rib tip at the top intact. The first thing we do is "peel" the ribs by removing the membrane that covers the bone side of the slab. The membrane makes the ribs tough to eat. Peeling off the membrane also allows more seasoning to get into the meat, from the rub to the sauce; in fact, the vinegar in the sauce doesn't just flavor the meat, but also tenderizes it.

Now, there's always going to be preferences within barbecue. Some people think the rib tips are too bony or too tough compared to the meat between the ribs—but I don't mind. I like the slight resistance you get when you bite into our ribs—I consider them perfect. That said, this recipe will work for St. Louis cut ribs (which have the rib tips removed) and tender, quicker cooking baby back ribs, too. For St. Louis cut, flip the ribs after 1 hour to 1 hour 15 minutes of cooking, while baby backs will be ready to turn after 30 to 45 minutes.

3 slabs pork spare ribs, membranes removed

1½ tablespoons Rib Rub (page 205)

2 to 3 cups Rodney's Sauce (page 211)

Fire up your grill to between 200°F and 250°F (see Grilling Technique, page 95).

Season each slab with the rib rub. Make sure you get under the flap, the little piece of meat that dangles on the bone side of the ribs.

Place the seasoned ribs on the grill grate bone-side down, with the fatty end toward the middle of the grill. The middle of the grill tends to be hotter, so that will ensure that the thicker part of the rib gets cooked properly. Close the grill and cook: You are looking for caramelization on the rib before you flip them. That should take about 1½ hours. Open the grill and look for caramelization on the bone.

If it's ready, use the mop-flip-mop method (see Box). Close the grill. Bring the grill back up to temperature between 200°F to 250°F. Cook the ribs until the second side gets that same caramelized look. To check doneness, we pick up a slab of ribs with a pair of tongs and check how much give there is. When you pick the slab up, it should sag or flop easily. If a slight tear develops in the meat between the bones, that's another sign of doneness.

Mop-Flip-Mop

We use this method for all meats. It goes like this:

1. Mop the visible side of the meat with sauce.

2. Flip the meat over.

3. Mop the meat again.

Steak Sandwich with Sautéed Onions

**MAKES
1 SANDWICH**

YOU can smoke a prime rib just for this sandwich or you can use your leftovers to create this wonder. If you are using freshly smoked rib eye for this recipe, then you will shave thin slices of the hot meat and top with the sautéed onions and cheese.

For the sautéed onions

¼ cup canola oil

1 large yellow onion, halved lengthwise and cut crosswise into ¼-inch-thick slices

1 teaspoon Rib Rub (page 205)

For the sandwich

4 ounces Smoked Prime Rib (page 97), thinly sliced

¼ cup Rodney's Sauce (page 211)

1 slice white American cheese, provolone, or Swiss cheese

1 Martin's potato roll (or similar soft sandwich roll)

2 tablespoons Duke's mayonnaise

1 crunchy iceberg lettuce leaf

1 thick slice tomato

Make the sautéed onions: In a sauté pan, heat the oil over medium-high heat. Once the oil is hot, add the onion. Stir occasionally so they don't stick or burn. Cook until the onion is tender and slightly caramelized, 10 to 12 minutes. Then season them with the rib rub. Transfer the onion to a medium bowl (don't clean the pan—you'll use it for the buns). You will have more onion than you need for the sandwich, store the rest in an airtight container in the refrigerator for up to 5 days.

Make the sandwich: Place the thinly sliced rib eye in a small, clean skillet set over medium-high heat. Cook until all the visible fat is rendered and the meat begins to crisp up around the edges, 1 to 2 minutes. Add the sauce and turn off the heat to let the sauce soak into the meat. Use tongs to arrange the meat into a tight square. Lay the cheese over the meat so it begins to melt.

Toast the roll cut-side down, preferably in the same hot pan you used to cook the onion, over medium-low heat until golden brown, about 2 minutes.

Spread the Duke's mayonnaise on both sides of the toasted roll. Use a spatula to transfer the meat and cheese to the bottom half of the roll. Top with the onions, lettuce, and tomato. Cover with the top half of the roll and serve.

BBQ Bacon Burgers

I am a man who loves a good burger. Growing up, Juliette Pasley served my favorite one at Pasley's Cafe. I'm not sure that it was so special. It might have been just a plain old cheeseburger, probably less than a quarter pound of beef, but when I think of happiness and burgers, that's the one I go back to.

At the restaurant, I developed what I call "burger sauce." It's the combination of 1,000 Island Dressing (page 144) and The Other Sauce (page 212). In this recipe, instead of combining them into one sauce, the dressings stay separate and then the burger gets finished off with the barbecue sauce.

For the sautéed onions

¼ cup canola oil

1 large yellow onion, cut into ¼-inch-thick slices

1 teaspoon Rib Rub (page 205)

For the burgers and peppers

2 pounds ground chuck

Canola oil, for the grill

4 jalapeño peppers

4 teaspoons Rib Rub (page 205)

1 cup shredded cheddar cheese (about 4 ounces)

4 slices white American cheese

4 Martin's potato rolls (or other soft sandwich buns)

½ cup Rodney's 1,000 Island Dressing (page 144)

4 slices thick-cut bacon, fried crisp and cut into 2-inch pieces

¼ cup The Other Sauce (page 212)

Make the sautéed onions: In a sauté pan, heat the oil over medium-high heat. Once the oil is hot, add the onion slices. Stir occasionally so they don't stick or burn. Cook until the onion is tender and slightly caramelized, 10 to 12 minutes. Then season it with the rib rub and set aside.

Fire up your grill (see Grilling Technique, page 95). Heat the grill to 225°F to 250°F.

Make the burgers: Divide the ground chuck into 8 equal portions (4 ounces each) and form each into a 1-inch-thick patty.

Char the peppers: Use grilling tongs to lightly brush the grill grate with a canola oil-soaked cloth. Place the jalapeños on the grill until evenly charred and black, turning them every 2 minutes for 10 to 12 minutes. While the peppers are still hot from the grill, place them in a bag and close it, or place them in a bowl and cover with plastic wrap. Allow the peppers to steam for about 5 minutes. Take the peppers out of the bag and use a spoon or gloved fingers to remove the skin. Discard the skin, stems, and seeds (and take care not to touch your face or eyes).

Crank the heat on the grill up to between 400°F and 450°F, by opening the vents three-fourths of the way for a few minutes. Once the temperature has risen, close the vents slightly to maintain temperature and avoid flare-ups.

Cook the burgers: Season both sides of the patties with the rib rub, place them on the grill and close the top. Cook until each side has developed a slight brown crust, and some dark grill marks, about 3 to 4 minutes per side. Put cheddar cheese on 4 of the patties and white American cheese on the remaining 4 patties.

Split and toast the potato rolls on the grill, flat side down, for 30 to 45 seconds, depending on your preference of doneness. Spread the 1,000 Island dressing on both the top and bottom buns. Stack a cheddar-topped burger on top of an American cheese-topped burger on each bun. Top with the sautéed onions, bacon, and The Other Sauce. Place the top bun on top and serve with the grilled jalapeños on the side.

Pork T-Bones

SERVES 4

THE bones divide these chops into two sections. The smaller, darker section is the tenderloin—the pork version of filet mignon. The larger, lighter, longer section is the loin. It has a little more chew and has a reputation of being a little dry. But after a few hours of dry brining in the refrigerator with rib rub and salt, this pork chop will be moist and well-seasoned all the way to the bone.

¼ cup Rib Rub
(page 205)

2 teaspoons Diamond
Crystal kosher salt

4 pork T-bone steaks
(8 ounces each),
1 inch thick

1 cup Rodney's Sauce
(page 211)

Canola oil, for the grill

Combine the rib rub and salt and mix thoroughly. Season the T-bones all over with the rib rub mixture, place them in a large zip-top bag, and refrigerate for 6 to 8 hours.

Remove the pork chops from the refrigerator to take off some of the chill before cooking, about 20 to 30 minutes.

Fire up your grill (see Grilling Technique, page 95). Heat the grill to between 400°F and 450°F.

Measure out ¼ cup of the sauce and place in small bowl for mopping. Set the rest of the sauce aside for serving.

Use grilling tongs to lightly brush the grill grate with a canola oil-soaked cloth. Place the T-bones on the grill and lightly mop with the sauce in the bowl. Close the grill and cook until the meat begins to develop nice deep brown grill marks, about 8 minutes. Flip, mop again, close the grill, and cook until the second side also has deep brown grill marks, about another 8 minutes. Stand the T-bone up on the bone side and cook covered until it is also nicely browned, about 4 minutes.

Remove the pork steaks from the grill and set on a platter. Allow to rest in the remaining sauce for at least 5 minutes before serving.

Honey-Butter Fish

MOST of the time fish is grilled or sautéed quickly over high heat. But if you cook a fish on a hot barbecue grill, it doesn't have a chance to pick up all the smoke flavor. So I came up with this recipe to take advantage of the smoke and to also play with the yin and yang of the salty rib rub and the sweet honey butter.

6 (6-ounce) skinless fish fillets, such as trout, catfish, red snapper, or branzino

2 tablespoons Rib Rub (page 205)

6 tablespoons Honey Butter (page 163)

Fire up your grill (see Grilling Technique, page 95). Heat the grill to between 225°F and 250°F.

Season the fish fillets with the rib rub. Cut pieces of foil big enough to fit each of your fish fillets lengthwise and then fold the foil into a sling so that it will nestle the fish and keep the melted butter from running into the coals. Place the empty foil slings on the grill (just the foil, you add the fish in a minute). Add ½ tablespoon of honey butter to each piece of foil. As the butter starts to melt, nestle each fish fillet on each piece of foil. Leave the foil open to allow maximum smoke flavor to get to the fish.

Close the grill and cook until the fish loses its translucent appearance and flakes easily when a fork is gently inserted, 30 to 35 minutes. Serve hot, with additional honey butter on the side.

Lemon and Herb Chicken

WHEN you think about putting meat on the grill, it automatically conjures up the standard barbecue sauces and sides. But if you think of smoke as one of the many flavors in barbecued meat, then you are free to imagine a totally different set of seasonings. This is one of my favorite combinations—it's simple and delicious, and a bit lighter in flavor thanks to a marinade made from a whole lot of lemon juice and a handful of bruised fresh oregano, rosemary, and thyme. I like to leave the proteins in larger pieces when I'm cooking on the grill. It makes it easier to turn them. For this recipe I split the chickens and cook the halves side by side. You can ask your butcher to split the birds for you if you don't trust your own knife skills. Also, if you'd prefer to have your chicken in smaller serving pieces, feel free to cut them up accordingly.

2 whole chickens (3 to 4 pounds each), spatchcocked or cut in half (see Tip)

1½ cups fresh lemon juice (from 6 to 8 lemons)

1 tablespoon Dijon mustard

½ cup olive oil

3 tablespoons Diamond Crystal kosher salt

1 tablespoon freshly ground black pepper

4 sprigs fresh oregano

4 sprigs fresh thyme

1 sprig fresh rosemary

Place the chickens in a large bowl or baking dish. Stack the halves if necessary.

In a medium bowl, whisk together the lemon juice and mustard until thoroughly combined. Continue whisking as you slowly drizzle in the olive oil to form an emulsified marinade (it should be thick and creamy). Add the salt and pepper and whisk again to combine.

Pour the marinade over the chickens. Using a mortar and pestle or the back of your chef's knife, press on the herbs (still on the stems) to "bruise" them, releasing some of their aromas and oils. Add the bruised herbs to the chickens. Toss the chickens in the marinade, making sure all parts are covered. Cover with plastic wrap and refrigerate for at least 1 hour and up to 1 hour 30 minutes. If you stacked the chicken, rearrange the pieces halfway through the marinating process so that the pieces on the top are rotated to the bottom.

Fire up your grill to between 250°F and 275°F (see Grilling Technique, page 95).

Remove the chickens from the marinade. Brush off any herbs that are still clinging to the meat so they won't burn on the grill. Load the meat onto the grill skin-side up. Close and cook until the bottom side of the chickens are well browned, about 1½ hours, maintaining a steady smoking temperature of between 225°F and 250°F.

Flip the chickens over. Close the grill, bring the temperature back up to 250°F, and cook until the thickest part of the meat registers 165°F, about 1 hour. Remove from the grill and transfer to a platter. Let the chickens rest 15 minutes before serving.

🔩 RODNEY'S PRO TIP
Have your butcher remove the backbones and spatchcock the chickens so the birds lie flat on the grill. Or, if you prefer, after removing the backbones, cut the chickens in half through the breastplate.

Smoked Turkey Breast

SMOKING the turkey breast separate from the whole turkey is definitely not traditional barbecue. But I'm less interested in traditional than I am in just plain good. Turkey absorbs smoke flavors very well. People who automatically turn their noses up at breast meat will have to think again after they taste this. Because there's so little fat on a turkey breast, I wrap it in foil after the first hour and a half of cooking. That keeps it from drying out. It'll already have plenty of color and smoke by then.

1 boneless, skin-on whole turkey breast (5 to 6 pounds)

3 tablespoons Rib Rub (page 205)

2 cups Rodney's Sauce (page 211)

Sprinkle the turkey breast with the rib rub. Place it uncovered in the refrigerator for 1 hour or so to let the spices permeate the meat.

Fire up your grill to between 225°F and 250°F (see Grilling Technique, page 95).

Place the turkey breast on the grill skin-side up. Close and cook, maintaining a steady temperature (see page 95), until the turkey takes on a deep tan color and gives slightly when pressed, about 1 hour and 30 minutes.

Remove the turkey breast from the grill and place it on a thick sheet of foil long enough to enclose the breast. Fold the foil up slightly around the edges so the sauce won't drip into the coals. Mop the turkey breast with the sauce, then close the foil around the turkey breast, using tongs to crimp the edges shut. Return to the grill, close the lid, and cook until the meat reaches an internal temperature of 165°F, another 1 hour 30 minutes.

Remove from the grill and allow the turkey to rest for 5 minutes before carving and serving.

Holiday Turkey

WHEN you cook a turkey on the pit the way we do, you don't end up with a pretty gold bird like the ones you see on the covers of the Thanksgiving issues of all the food magazines. But I don't think most of those pretty birds taste as good as one that's been smoked on the pit or grill and seasoned the way we do. Spatch-cocking the turkey allows us to cook it more evenly and get seasoning throughout the bird. You be the judge.

1 whole turkey (12 to 14 pounds), giblets removed (save for gravy or discard), and spatchcocked (see Tip)

½ cup Rib Rub (page 205)

4 cups Rodney's Sauce (page 211)

Fire up your grill to 250°F (see Grilling Technique, page 95).

Prepare the turkey by sprinkling rib rub all over both sides of the bird. Place the turkey on the grill grate skin-side down, close the grill, and cook for 1 hour 30 minutes.

Using a small, clean mop or a basting brush, baste the turkey with the sauce. Flip the turkey so it's skin-side up and baste the skin side. Close the grill and cook until the thickest part of the thigh meat registers 160°F, another 1 hour 30 minutes. (Once you have finished basting the turkey, discard any remaining sauce, as it will have come into contact with raw turkey.)

Remove the turkey from the grill and let it rest for 30 to 40 minutes before carving and transferring to a platter.

🐷 **RODNEY'S PRO TIP**

Spatchcocking the turkey allows it to lie flat on the grill. Have your butcher do this, or to do it yourself: Set the turkey breast-side down on your work surface, with the tail facing you. Using a pair of kitchen shears, cut up from the tail to the neck on each side of the backbone. Remove the backbone and save for soup or discard. If you prefer, at this point, you can cut the turkey in half through the breastplate.

Rodney's Wings

SERVES 4 TO 6

I knew I wanted to have chicken wings on the menu and I knew I wanted to do something different from the fried wings that are on every sports bar menu from coast to coast. The obvious thing was to put them in our pits to get that flavor on them and then fry them for that wing-crispy crunch everybody loves. The first couple of times we tried it, we smoked the wings too long. They came out of the fryer dry. We finally found the sweet spot by smoking them for about 30 minutes and then chilling them until just before time to serve them. Then, after a quick fry, they're just right.

When you're planning the timing of your meal, don't forget that these wings need to be refrigerated for 1 hour before they are fried and served.

2 to 5 pounds chicken wings, split into drumettes and flats (leave the wing tip attached to the flats if you choose)

2 to 5 tablespoons Rib Rub (1 tablespoon per pound of wings; page 205)

2 cups canola or other vegetable oil, for frying

Fire up your grill to between 225°F and 250°F (see Grilling Technique, page 95).

Pat the wings dry with paper towels and season them with half of the rib rub. Place the wings directly on the grill grate, spreading them out so they do not overlap. Close and cook the wings until the smoke and rub have rendered them a deep red color, almost maroon, about 30 minutes. Be careful not to overcook the wings or they'll be dry after they are fried. Remove the wings from the grill, allow to cool completely, then refrigerate for at least 1 hour.

Add the oil to a cast-iron skillet to fill it about 2 inches deep and heat it to 375°F. Working in batches to avoid overcrowding the pan, use tongs to transfer the wings to the oil. Fry the wings until they are golden brown on both sides, 2 to 3 minutes, flipping regularly, to ensure even cooking.

Use a slotted spoon or frying spider to transfer the cooked wings from the skillet to a large bowl and toss them with a few sprinkles of the remaining rib rub. Repeat with the remaining wings and serve.

Smoked Chicken

SERVES 4 TO 6

WE raised chickens for their eggs when I was a boy. The difference between fresh-laid eggs and store-bought eggs is huge. Yard eggs are richer in flavor, and when you beat them, they even seem thicker in texture. We would buy chicken at the market to eat, rather than slaughter our laying hens. My mother used to make what we called "barbecue chicken" in the oven. It was basically baked chicken with commercial barbecue sauce. I don't want to knock it. I enjoyed that baked chicken, but I wouldn't call it barbecue. It wasn't until later, when we added chicken to the menu at the family restaurant that I got into true smoked chicken. The oven and the pit are very different, obviously. When you taste this chicken, you'll have a hard time going back to your oven.

2 whole chickens (3 to 4 pounds each), spatchcocked (see Tip, page 114) and halved through the breastplate (a total of 4 halves)

3 tablespoons Rib Rub (page 205)

4 cups Rodney's Sauce (page 211)

Fire up your grill to between 225°F and 250°F (see Grilling Technique, page 95).

Sprinkle the chickens on all sides with the rib rub. Place the chicken onto the hot grill, bone-side down. Close and cook until the bone sides are nicely browned, about 1 hour and 30 minutes, being careful to maintain a steady grilling temperature between 225°F and 250°F.

Mop the skin side with the sauce, then flip the chickens and mop the bone side with sauce as well. Close and cook until the thickest part of the thigh reaches 165°F, about 1 hour.

Mop the chickens once more. Take them off the grill and allow them to rest for 5 minutes before serving.

FROM TH

E STOVE

Chicken Perloo | SERVES 4

THIS is my favorite one-pot recipe. It's great as a side dish or a center table item. We use chicken in this recipe, but you could substitute another protein such as shrimp or pork. When Paul, the culinary director for the whole Pihakis Restaurant Group, first tasted perloo he said it reminded him of a *caldoso*, a Spanish soupy rice dish.

¼ cup olive oil

6 celery stalks, cut into ¼-inch pieces (about 1½ cups)

1 large green bell pepper, cut into ¼-inch pieces

1 medium yellow onion, cut into ¼-inch pieces

2 tablespoons finely chopped garlic

1 (14.5-ounce) can stewed tomatoes

2 teaspoons Rib Rub (page 205)

1 teaspoon Diamond Crystal kosher salt

6 cups chicken stock (see Tip)

1 cup short-grain rice, such as Charleston Gold or Arborio

12 ounces smoked chicken meat (page 118), picked off the bone (roughly half of a bird)

1 bunch scallions, chopped, for garnish

Preheat the oven to 350°F.

In a Dutch oven, heat the oil over medium heat. Add the celery, bell pepper, onion, and garlic and cook until the vegetables become translucent and soft, about 15 minutes.

Add the stewed tomatoes, rib rub, and salt to the sautéed vegetables and cook until all the liquid is gone and the mixture begins to caramelize on the bottom of the pot, about 15 minutes.

Add the stock and bring to a boil. Stir in the rice and smoked chicken and transfer to the oven. Bake uncovered until the rice is soft and cooked through, about 20 minutes. Then the dish is done. Remove from the oven and garnish with the scallions.

RODNEY'S PRO TIP
If you have some leftover potlikker (the liquid leftover after you cook a pot of greens or beans) use that instead of chicken stock.

Coco's Pigtail Perloo

My wife's name is Shanika. When we first started dating, I took to calling her Coco. I told her I did that because she was brown and sweet. I also called her that because I'm better at remembering nicknames than I am at remembering names.

When I started putting together this book, I told my wife that it wouldn't just include recipes from the restaurant. There would also be some family recipes as well. I told her that I always love her pigtail perloo. That's the kind of recipe you're not going to see in a lot of cookbooks and it says a lot about me and where I'm from and the woman I chose to marry. When I pressed her about writing down the recipe, she shrugged and gave me a noncommittal answer. I asked again and she shrugged again.

One day I came home and Coco had a pot of pigtail perloo on the stove. "I thought you were going to let me write down the recipe while you cooked it." She shrugged and gave me a noncommittal answer.

That, ladies and gentlemen, is my wife.

We dated for about four years, and I still didn't learn my lesson. I asked her to marry me. We tied the knot in 2015. Nick was my best man.

My wife chooses not to put our business out on Front Street, as the old folks say. She worked in the schools for years, but she works at the restaurant now. She chooses not to travel with me most of the time. She'd rather stay home and raise our son, Braylon.

She has a crazy sense of humor and sometimes our conversations sound off the wall, like the things couples might say to each other on sitcoms. That's what makes being married to her fun.

What makes her my partner, my ride or die, my rock, is the way she stood by me through all the things I went through with my family early in our courtship. For that, I will forever be grateful.

For those of you interested in a recipe for pigtail perloo, you'll have to ask her yourself.

Fried Chicken

MOST everybody's mom made good fried chicken, but my mom made *really good* fried chicken. She told me that the keys were seasoning the flour as well as the chicken, and making sure the grease was hot before you put the chicken in. Every now and then, she would use my grandmother's method—and then the chicken would go from *really good* to *really special*.

Here's what made grandmother's fried chicken stand out: After we flipped a hog on the pit, she'd collect the grease that would bubble up in the cavity. That grease was seasoned with all the vinegar and pepper from the barbecue sauce. She'd let the seasoned fat cool so it would become solid, like cooled bacon fat. There wouldn't be enough to fry a whole chicken, but if you added some vegetable oil to it, you'd get a fried chicken with flavor that was out of this world.

I've heard that the legendary chef Edna Lewis brined her chicken in buttermilk and then fried it in lard seasoned with butter and country ham. In a way, I suppose that's similar to my grandmother's method of seasoning the oil. These days when I fry chicken, I don't season the oil. But like Ms. Lewis, I do brine the bird for at least a few hours. That way you get flavor all the way to the bone. And if you wanted to add some cooled bacon fat or hog drippings to the fry oil, well, your chicken will be all the better for it.

1 cup Rib Rub (page 205)

2 whole chickens
(3 pounds each), each
cut up into 8 pieces

2 cups all-purpose flour

2 tablespoons Diamond
Crystal kosher salt

2 tablespoons freshly
ground black pepper

Canola or other vegetable
oil, for frying

In a medium saucepan, bring 4 cups water to a boil. Add the rib rub and stir until fully dissolved. Transfer the mixture to a large container or pot (like a canning pot) and add 8 more cups water and 4 cups ice. Refrigerate until the brine is well chilled, then add the chicken pieces and refrigerate at least 6 and up to 8 hours.

Remove the chicken from the refrigerator and allow it to come to room temperature. In a large bowl or brown paper bag, combine the flour, salt, and pepper. Place the chicken, a few pieces at a time, into the seasoned flour. Close the bag and shake it to thoroughly coat the chicken parts with the flour. Repeat until all of the chicken has been coated. (The chicken will still be wet from the brine. That's okay. More coating will cling to the chicken and help to form an extra-crispy crust.)

Set a cooling rack over a sheet pan. Pour enough oil into a large Dutch oven or cast-iron pan to fill it 3 inches and heat to between 350°F and 365°F on an instant-read thermometer.

Working in batches to avoid crowding, add the chicken to the oil, taking care to cook pieces of a similar size so they'll be done at the same time. Cook the chicken until the side that is submerged in the oil is golden brown, about 8 minutes for smaller pieces and 10 minutes for the larger pieces. Using a slotted spoon or a frying spider, turn the pieces over and cook until golden brown or until the thickest part of the meat reaches 165°F, another 8 to 10 minutes. Transfer the chicken to the cooling rack on the sheet pan. Cook more batches, making sure to bring the oil back up to 350°F before adding the next batch.

Serve hot or at room temperature.

Fried Catfish

SOMEBODY always had a line in the water when I was coming up. We ate a lot of croaker, Florida brim, and catfish—and I don't really remember eating fish any other way but fried. My grandmother made the best fried catfish—crispy, tender, and slightly salty. If we didn't catch anything or if nobody gave us a few extra fish from their catch, we'd buy it from Laurie "Fish Man" Cooper, who had the fish market in town. Laurie also happens to know how to cook a hog—he even cooked with me at the Big Apple Block Party in New York City one year. But this recipe is about catfish, not whole hog—and this recipe is the closest I have come to getting the flavors of my grandmother's fried catfish.

2 cups cornmeal, preferably fine ground

1 cup all-purpose flour

1 teaspoon Diamond Crystal kosher salt

2 teaspoons MSG (Jesus's Tears, see page 208)

1 teaspoon freshly ground black pepper

2 teaspoons cayenne pepper

3 pounds catfish fillets

4 cups vegetable oil, for frying

In a bowl, combine the cornmeal, flour, salt, 1 teaspoon of the MSG, the black pepper, and 1 teaspoon of the cayenne. Mix until thoroughly combined. Coat the catfish fillets in the cornmeal mixture, making sure both sides are completely covered.

Set a cooling rack on a sheet pan. Add enough oil to a large cast-iron skillet to fill it by 2 inches and heat over medium-high heat to 350°F.

Working in batches to avoid crowding, gently add the catfish, a few fillets at a time, and fry until golden brown on the bottom, 3 to 4 minutes. Carefully flip the fillets and cook until golden brown on the second side, another 3 to 4 minutes. Transfer the batches to the cooling rack as you work.

In a small bowl, combine the remaining 1 teaspoon MSG and 1 teaspoon cayenne. Sprinkle this over the catfish while they are still hot.

Pork and Grits

BACK in Hemingway, early in the morning, you would get people coming by the pit on their way to work. We weren't even open. But they would ask me if any of the pork was ready. If I had something ready, they'd say, "Fix me a half pound," or they might say, "Let me get my grits, and I'll be right back."

At first I wondered where they were running to get these grits from. I found out they were going to Hardee's, the fast-food place, buying an order of grits, and coming back to the pit for some pork. This would go on just about every week, especially when the weather was cold. I didn't even have the scale set up at that hour. So I would just eyeball the weight and charge them whatever I thought the price would be.

When we opened Rodney Scott's Whole Hog BBQ in Charleston we put pork and grits on the menu. The recipe we came up with tasted great. I could see why people were coming out to the pit in Hemingway in the morning to get their fix. The problem we had at the restaurant was that most people thought of grits as a morning thing. Even though Low Country shrimp and grits are taking menus by storm all over the country, people around Charleston couldn't seem to quite get their heads around grits and pork for lunch or dinner. So we had to take it off the menu.

Sometimes in the morning, I still like to pull a little piece of meat off of the belly area or around the ribs and make myself a breakfast pork sandwich. In terms of pork and grits, the way I like to do it now is several steps above the Hardee's grits folks were buying.

I use stone-ground grits, which taste great. They have a chewier texture and a richer flavor than commercial grits. Sometimes with the supermarket grits, you can't really even taste that they are made from corn. You might mistake them for Cream of Wheat. You'd never make that mistake with artisan stone-ground grits.

The recipe I came up with is great for breakfast. But don't get it twisted. It tastes great for lunch, dinner, or any other time of the day.

For the cheese grits

4 cups whole milk

2 cups stone-ground yellow grits (Anson Mills or Geechie Boy Mill)

1 stick (4 ounces) unsalted butter, cut into 4 pieces

1 cup grated cheddar cheese (see Tip)

1 tablespoon Diamond Crystal kosher salt

1 teaspoon Texas Pete hot sauce

For serving

1½ pounds chopped, pulled, or sliced barbecued pork

½ cup Rodney's Sauce (page 211)

½ cup store-bought pork skins, crumbled

Make the cheese grits: In a Dutch oven or large saucepan, combine the milk and 4 cups water and bring to a simmer over medium-high heat. Stir occasionally to prevent the milk from scorching. Slowly pour in the grits and stir with a whisk so they don't clump together. Reduce the heat to medium-low and cook, stirring occasionally to prevent the bottom from burning, until the grits are fully cooked and tender, 1 hour to 1 hour 30 minutes.

Stir in the butter and cheddar. Season the grits with the salt and hot sauce.

To serve: Spoon 1 cup of cheese grits into each bowl or plate. Top with 4 ounces of barbecued pork, a splash of Rodney's sauce, and some crumbled pork skins.

🧀 RODNEY'S PRO TIP
It's best to grate your own cheese rather than buy pre-grated cheese from the supermarket. That cheese has cornstarch added to keep it from sticking together.

SNACKS,
& VEGE

SALADS,
TABLES

Pork Skins, Pork Rinds, Cracklins & Chicharrones

If you go to a filling station along any highway in America you'll probably see bags of puffed pork products. Sometimes they'll say "pork skins." Sometimes they'll say "pork rinds." Usually they are the same thing: the fatty part of the pig, fried or baked until it's airy and crispy.

If you're in the South, you might also see bags of cracklins, which is fried pork that includes the skin, fat, and a little meat from the hog. If you're lucky enough to have a Latin market where you are, you might see freshly made chicharrones being sold behind the butcher's counter. These are more or less the same thing as the cracklins I grew up on.

In the old days, when I was working with my parents in Hemingway, we would crisp the skin of the hogs we had barbecued and sell it until we ran out or it got too soft to sell. After a few hours in humid weather or a day or two in general, it was difficult to get the skin crispy again. Even so, some customers would still buy it because they liked the chewiness of it, or they'd take it to season a pot of greens. Eventually, we started frying it and selling it in bags. But it was still hard to get the volume and consistent quality of pork skins we needed to make it really viable for us.

One day, a salesman who was selling us spices mentioned these commercial pork skin pellets and suggested that we try them. I'd never seen or heard of anything like that. The best description I can come up with is that they looked like dehydrated pork skins. They kind of had the color and texture of pork skins, but they were small and dry. We tried them. They just crisped right up and the flavor was amazing. When it came time to open in Charleston, I went back to those pork skins for the menu. The customers really took to them—they were ordering pork skins like they were going out of style! That's when I knew that there would be no stopping us—we were really going to be a success in Charleston.

We get our pork skin pellets from American Skin (pork-rinds.com). We use two kinds of cracklins and they sell them both. Their "selects" are like the commercial pig skins you find in stores next to the potato chips and other snacks. They're light and fluffy. They're the ones Angie Mosier uses for her cake (see Angie Mo's Cracklin' Layer Cake, page 177) and they'd also be good to serve alongside Paul Yeck's Smoked Catfish Dip (opposite).

American Skins doesn't sell them in small enough quantities for home use, but you can find other sources online that will sell smaller amounts—for example from Bourque's Super Store in Port Barre, Louisiana (bourquespecialties.com). Or look for Carolina Gold Nuggets, which are available from various online retailers.

For the recipes in this book that call for cracklins, I recommend that you buy a bag of plain, commercial pork rinds. There are several good options. My friends at 4505 Burgers & BBQ Restaurant make an excellent version that is sold nationally. Epic Provisions makes a baked version that's good. Whatever version you like will work.

The "hard cracklins" from American Skin have more fat and a little skin and meat attached as well. Those are more like the pork skins we would make from the skins of the pigs we cooked. I don't know of anyone who sells those pellets in small enough quantities for most home use. If you're craving those, your best option is to look for chicharrones in a Latin supermarket in your area.

Paul Yeck's Smoked Catfish Dip

SERVES 8 TO 10 AS AN APPETIZER

PAUL YECK is the chief cook of our parent company, the Pihakis Restaurant Group. He was in the kitchen one day trying to figure out what we were going to cook for a fundraiser for the Jones Valley Teaching Farm in Birmingham. Smoked fish is a staple in Southern coastal communities. Instead of the smoked mullet you might find in other places, Paul came up with the idea of using smoked catfish. When I tasted the dip, I was like "This is amazing." It's just unbelievably good. Ever since that day, we've been serving this at special events with some pork skins alongside for dipping. We've also served this with hushpuppies. Paul calls it Rodney's surf and turf.

1 pound catfish fillets

4 tablespoons Rib Rub (page 205)

1 to 2 celery stalks, cut into ¼-inch dice (about ½ cup)

3 to 4 scallions, white and tender green parts, chopped (about ½ cup)

¾ cup Duke's mayonnaise

Grated zest and juice of 1 lemon

Toast points, crackers, hushpuppies, or pork skins, for dipping

Fire up your grill to between 225°F and 250°F (see Grilling Technique, page 95).

Season the catfish fillets on both sides with 2 tablespoons of the rib rub. Lay the fillets on the grill grate, close the grill, and cook until the fish is cooked through. It will appear opaque and will flake apart easily when prodded with a fork, 35 to 45 minutes.

Remove the fish from the grill and allow it to cool completely, about 30 minutes.

Using your fingers, break the catfish into small pieces and place them in a medium bowl. Add the celery, scallions, mayonnaise, lemon zest, and lemon juice and stir. Add the remaining 2 tablespoons rib rub and fold all the ingredients until thoroughly combined.

Serve with toast points, crackers, or hushpuppies. Or best of all, for a surf and turf appetizer, serve with pork skins.

SERVES 4 TO 6

Loaded Pork Skin "Nachos"

I know you've had fried tortilla chips with cheese and hot peppers. And I know you've had stuffed potato skins. But believe me, pork skin nachos are on another level. These are as rich as can be, but worth every calorie.

3 ounces pork skins
(1 medium bag)

¼ cup grated cheddar
cheese

½ cup shredded or
chopped barbecued
pork (or any other
smoked meat),
warmed through

¼ cup Kathy's Sweet
Sauce (page 215) or
Rodney's White Barbecue
Sauce (page 214)

1 tablespoon Crispy
Bacon Bits (page 216)

2 tablespoons thinly
sliced scallion (white and
green parts)

2 heaping tablespoons
sour cream

Position a rack in the center of the oven and preheat the oven to 425°F.

Arrange the pork skins on a sheet pan large enough to hold them and top with the cheddar and the meat. Transfer to the oven for just long enough to melt the cheese, 5 to 7 minutes.

Remove from the oven and top with the sauce, bacon bits, scallions, and sour cream. Serve hot.

Pimento Cheese

SERVES 8 TO 10
AS AN APPETIZER

PIMENTO cheese is one of those foods that everyone associates with the South. The South isn't the only place where people thought of putting pimiento peppers and cheese together. But the South is the only place where the dish became so legendary. The first time I ever tried it was when I was in elementary school. The cafeteria served us a pimento cheese sandwich alongside a bowl of tomato soup. The tomato soup I didn't like—I gave that away. The pimento cheese sandwich, though, was something else: It was new. It was different. I wasn't sure if I liked it or not. But I kept eating it, nibbling off of it a little at a time. So many of my chef friends make it, and I've had so many good versions, that it's really grown on me. My favorite way to eat it is, of course, on pork skins—or layered onto a BLT for a BLTPC.

1 pound sharp cheddar cheese (yellow is traditional, but white is fine)

8 ounces cream cheese, at room temperature

1 cup Duke's mayonnaise

1 cup jarred diced pimientos, drained

3 tablespoons Rib Rub (page 205)

1 teaspoon Colman's mustard powder

1 teaspoon onion powder

3 ounces pork skins (1 medium bag) or celery stalks, for serving

Using a box grater, shred the cheddar on the medium shredding holes into a medium bowl. In a large bowl, mix together the cream cheese and mayonnaise. Add the pimientos, rib rub, mustard powder, and onion powder, mixing until blended. Fold in the grated cheddar, making sure it is evenly incorporated.

Transfer to a serving bowl and serve as a dip with pork skins or celery stalks. Pimento cheese can be refrigerated in an airtight container for up to 1 week.

🍀 **RODNEY'S PRO TIP**
Don't use preshredded cheese. It's coated with cornstarch to prevent it from clumping. Only freshly grated cheese will give you the creamy result you're looking for.

Marinated Tomatoes and Onions

SERVES 4 TO 6

SUMMER means tomatoes to me, whether I'm talking about the old days when we grew our own in the garden, or these days when I see them in the farmers' market. When they're at the peak of ripeness, the less you do to them, the better. Depending on the variety of tomato you use, the flavor will be some combination of sweet, tangy, and salty. That's the same combination in the dressing here. There's a little sugar in both the vinaigrette and the rib rub for the sweetness. That helps heighten the sweetness of the tomatoes and onion. The tang of the vinegar and the brightness of the salt all combine to enhance what nature already did flavorwise.

3 medium tomatoes (about 1 pound)

½ medium sweet onion, such as Vidalia or Walla Walla, cut into ¼-inch-wide strips

1 teaspoon Diamond Crystal kosher salt

⅓ cup Rodney's Vinaigrette (recipe follows)

¼ cup loosely packed basil leaves, torn into medium-sized pieces

2 teaspoons Rib Rub (page 205)

Wash and core the tomatoes. Cut them however you wish—into slices, wedges, or chunks—and place them in a medium bowl.

Add the onion, salt, and vinaigrette and gently toss until the tomatoes are coated evenly. Set the mixture aside to macerate at room temperature for about 10 minutes. This will help to soften the onions slightly; it will help draw out the natural juices in the tomatoes and it will allow the flavors to marry.

Right before serving, add the basil and the rib rub. Toss together and serve.

RODNEY'S VINAIGRETTE

Makes about 1¼ cups

½ cup Rodney's Sauce (page 211)
2 teaspoons Dijon mustard
¾ cup extra-virgin olive oil
1 teaspoon Diamond Crystal kosher salt

In a small bowl, whisk together Rodney's sauce and the mustard. While whisking, slowly drizzle in the olive oil to create a creamy emulsion. Add the salt and whisk until it is thoroughly incorporated. Use immediately or store in a screw-top jar in the refrigerator for up to 1 month. Shake vigorously before use.

John T. Wedge Salad

JOHN T. EDGE was the one man who came and saw what we were doing in Hemingway and who *understood* what we were doing in Hemingway. To just look at him, you would think he was just some regular, run-of-the-mill white boy from south Georgia, but the dude is straight-up cool. Calm under pressure and so confident in his knowledge that he can be cool about it (unlike others who have to show off all the time). This wedge salad, made with a chilled wedge of iceberg and homemade 1,000 Island dressing, is like John—just cool. When John first came to Scott's Pit Cook B.B.Q., he wasn't like a lot of journalists who come in, get enough information for their article, and then leave. We spent real time together and the article he wrote for the *New York Times* became the basis for our friendship. Over the years we've talked often and spent time traveling together. People trust him when he says that this or that food is good, and as a result we've gotten a lot of customers over the years from his recommendation. It felt good to honor him by putting his name on the menu.

1 head iceberg lettuce

¾ cup Rodney's 1,000 Island Dressing (recipe follows)

¼ cup Crispy Bacon Bits (page 216)

2 scallions, white and green parts, thinly sliced (about ¼ cup)

½ teaspoon Rib Rub (page 205)

¼ cup crumbled pork skins (optional)

12 cherry tomatoes, halved

Remove any dirty or wilted outside leaves from the lettuce. Cut the head into quarters, cut out the core and place each quarter on a plate. Drizzle each lettuce wedge with dressing, then sprinkle each wedge with bacon, scallions, a pinch of rib rub, and pork skins (if using). Scatter the tomatoes around the lettuce and serve.

RODNEY'S 1,000 ISLAND DRESSING
Makes about 2 cups

¾ cup Duke's mayonnaise

½ cup Kathy's Sweet Sauce (page 215)

½ cup Rodney's White Barbecue Sauce (page 214)

¼ cup sweet pickle relish

1 tablespoon Rib Rub (page 205)

In a bowl, combine the mayo, sweet sauce, white barbecue sauce, pickle relish, and rib rub. Thoroughly mix. The dressing can be refrigerated in an airtight container for up to 2 weeks.

Coleslaw

WHEN Nick and I started to put together the menu, he picked my brain for the flavors and recipes I grew up on. Since coleslaw and barbecue are such a natural combination, I think he was hoping I had some old family recipe to draw from. But my childhood memories of coleslaw involved watching my mother eat it while I ate the barbecue or the fried fish it was served with. We developed a coleslaw recipe anyway, because the food at Rodney Scott's BBQ has to please people other than Rodney Scott.

Something has happened to me in the years since we opened, though. Every morning we taste all the food to make sure it's consistent. Tasting the coleslaw right before or right after the pork taught me something. The creaminess and the sweetness of the coleslaw goes perfectly with the vinegar and spice of my barbecue. In doing those tastings every morning, I fooled around and converted myself to coleslaw. Make a batch of this to go with your barbecue and I think you'll understand.

1 small head green cabbage (about 1½ pounds)

1 medium carrot

1 large green bell pepper

1 cup Duke's mayonnaise

¼ cup sweet pickle relish

2 tablespoons red wine vinegar

2 tablespoons sugar

2 teaspoons Diamond Crystal kosher salt

½ teaspoon freshly ground black pepper

⅛ teaspoon cayenne pepper

Cut the cabbage head into quarters and remove the tough core. Use a box grater (or the grating attachment of a food processor) to grate the cabbage and then the carrot. Place them in a large bowl. Cut the green pepper into ¼-inch dice and add them to the bowl.

In a small bowl, combine the mayonnaise, relish, vinegar, sugar, salt, black pepper, and cayenne. Mix thoroughly and pour the dressing over the vegetables. Toss until the cabbage is fully dressed. Serve immediately or refrigerate in an airtight container and serve within 3 to 4 days.

Potato Salad

SERVES 8 TO 10

SOMETIMES we'd have potato salad with Sunday dinner, but mostly we had it as a barbecue side dish. It was definitely one of my favorites. Still is. I think it's the sweet-spicy-sour interplay between the sweet pickles, the mayonnaise, and the mustard that I like so much. Using red-skinned potatoes gives you a creamier result than russet potatoes. It's best to dress the potatoes when they're still hot. That not only gets the seasoning into the potatoes quicker, it also creates a balanced texture for a mighty fine potato salad.

For the potatoes

1¾ teaspoons Diamond Crystal kosher salt

3½ pounds red-skinned potatoes, skin on, washed and quartered

For the dressing

2 cups Duke's mayonnaise

¼ cup yellow mustard (French's or whatever you prefer)

½ cup distilled white vinegar

¼ cup fresh lemon juice

½ cup sweet pickle relish

1 tablespoon Diamond Crystal kosher salt

2 teaspoons sugar

2 teaspoons freshly ground black pepper

½ teaspoon red pepper flakes

¼ teaspoon cayenne pepper

½ cup finely diced celery (1 to 2 stalks)

½ cup finely diced red onion (about 1 medium onion)

For the salad

4 hard-boiled eggs, peeled

1½ tablespoons Rib Rub (page 205)

¼ cup thinly sliced scallions (optional), white and green parts (about 2 scallions)

Cook the potatoes: Bring a large saucepan of water to a boil. Add the salt and quartered potatoes. Reduce the heat and gently boil the potatoes until they yield easily when a knife is inserted through their centers, 15 to 20 minutes.

While the potatoes are cooking, make the dressing: In a large bowl, combine the mayo, mustard, vinegar, lemon juice, relish, salt, sugar, black pepper, pepper flakes, and cayenne and mix until incorporated. Whisk in the celery and red onion. Taste and adjust the seasoning if needed.

Make the salad: Once the potatoes are tender, drain them and add them (while hot) to the bowl with the dressing. Use a large spoon to break up the potatoes to really get the dressing into everything while the potatoes are hot.

Chop the eggs to your liking or press them through a sieve to break them up into fine bits. Fold the eggs into the salad. Finish the salad with a sprinkle of rib rub and the sliced scallions (if using).

Grilled Vegetable Salad

SERVES 4 TO 6

THE best way to make this salad is to go to the farmers' market and pick the vegetables that strike your fancy. Pretty much any vegetables will work. The trick is remembering that they require different amounts of time on the grill. Root vegetables tend to take the longest. I like how the grill encourages the vegetables to caramelize without overcooking them—plus all that smoky flavor is always a good thing.

1 large red bell pepper

3 tablespoons canola oil

2½ teaspoons Diamond Crystal kosher salt

1¼ teaspoons freshly ground black pepper

1 bunch baby carrots, tops trimmed (real baby carrots, not those weird little things that aren't even shaped like carrots)

1 medium yellow squash, quartered lengthwise and then halved crosswise

1 medium zucchini, cut into ½-inch rounds

1 bunch asparagus, woody ends snapped off

1 bunch scallions, root ends trimmed

½ cup Rodney's Vinaigrette (page 143)

1 teaspoon Rib Rub (page 205)

Fire up your grill to 400° to 450°F. See Grilling Technique (page 95).

In a medium bowl, toss the whole bell pepper with 2 teaspoons of the oil, ½ teaspoon of the salt, and ¼ teaspoon of the pepper. Place the whole pepper on the grill. (Keep the bowl for the rest of the vegetables.) As the pepper chars and blisters, use grilling tongs to turn it frequently so that the pepper gets charred on all sides—this will take 8 to 12 minutes. Remove it from the grill and immediately place it in a small paper or plastic bag. Close the bag and allow the pepper to steam for at least 5 minutes. Remove the pepper from the bag and use a spoon or gloved finger to remove the skin. Remove the seeds and stem, cut the roasted pepper into strips, and transfer them to a large bowl.

Place the carrots in the same bowl used to season the bell pepper. Toss them with 4 teaspoons of the oil, 1 teaspoon of the salt, and ½ teaspoon of the pepper. Place them on the grill (perpendicular to the grates).

Add the squash and zucchini to the bowl you used for the carrots and toss with 1½ teaspoons of the canola oil, ½ teaspoon of the salt, and ¼ teaspoon of the pepper. Once the carrots have been on the grill for 4 to 5 minutes, they should be brown and wrinkled and their thin tips might be almost black. Flip them. Place the squash and zucchini on the grill. Cook for another 5 to 6 minutes.

Toss the asparagus and scallions with the remaining 1½ teaspoons oil, ½ teaspoon salt, and ¼ teaspoon pepper. Place the asparagus and scallions on the grill, turning and rotating so that they cook evenly. Once they have a slight char and wrinkled skin, after 6 to 8 minutes, begin removing the vegetables as they are done and place them in the bowl with the roasted peppers. Toss the vegetables with the vinaigrette and transfer to a serving platter. Sprinkle with the rib rub and serve warm.

Coco's Smoked Chicken Salad

SERVES 2

NOT long after I met Coco, we were on a date and CeeLo Green came on the iPod singing "Fool for You." We both liked the song so much that we just played it over and over. One day in the restaurant, I put that song on while she was walking through. She immediately stopped and just started dancing. I love it when she does that. From the start, I always wanted Rodney Scott's Whole Hog BBQ to be a family restaurant—not just welcoming for families as guests, but reflecting the warmth and fun you get at family gatherings. Part of that for me meant putting the names of family members on the menu so that even when they weren't in the restaurant, they'd be there with me. Coco's Smoked Chicken Salad has a nice ring to it—I like the way it sounds. Plus my wife loves making egg salad, so I thought it wasn't much of a stretch to put her name on this dish—especially one that is, to me, one of the best things you can eat. When I'm cooking at home, sometimes I'll even put extra chicken on the pit hoping for leftovers so I can make it into salad.

When I told her about her namesake, she gave me one of those trademark Coco looks like I was out of my mind. But we went ahead with it, and she hasn't complained.

2 cups shredded pit-smoked chicken meat (from about ¼ to ½ of a Smoked Chicken, page 118), yesterday's leftovers are best!

1 celery stalk, cut into ¼-inch dice (about ⅓ cup)

½ medium yellow onion, cut into ¼-inch dice (about ⅓ cup)

1 cup Duke's mayonnaise

⅓ cup Rodney's Sauce (page 211)

1 tablespoon Rib Rub (page 205)

½ bunch scallions, white and green parts, sliced crosswise ¼ inch thick

Iceberg lettuce and sliced perfectly ripe tomatoes for serving, or sliced white bread for sandwiches

In a large bowl, combine the chicken, celery, onion, mayonnaise, Rodney's sauce, rib rub, and scallions. Combine everything thoroughly. It will last 3 or 4 days in the refrigerator.

Serve cold on a bed of iceberg lettuce with sliced tomatoes on the side. Or serve it as a sandwich on fresh white bread.

Pork Belly Succotash

SERVES 4 TO 6

MY mother's mother used to put up colorful jars of succotash during the summer when there were so many vegetables coming out of the garden that you couldn't eat them all. Rodney, the finicky kid, didn't eat many of them. Still this dish reminds me of her and the good times I had at her house watching TV and playing with my cousins.

1 pound cooked pork belly meat and fat (see Tip), preferably from a barbecued hog (see Cooking the Hog, page 83)

½ medium yellow onion, diced

1 teaspoon chopped garlic

4 ears corn, shucked, kernels shaved off the cob

1 pound fresh or frozen baby lima beans

2 cups meat or vegetable stock or water

½ cup heavy cream

1 tablespoon Diamond Crystal kosher salt

1 teaspoon Hog Seasoning (page 202)

4 tablespoons unsalted butter

1 medium tomato, diced, or ½ cup halved grape tomatoes

Chop the belly meat and fat. In a medium saucepan or Dutch oven, heat the meat over medium-high heat to render most of the fat, 3 to 5 minutes. Add the onion and garlic and cook, stirring occasionally, until translucent, 5 to 7 minutes. Add the corn and sauté until just tender, about 3 minutes. Add the lima beans and mix well.

Add the stock to the pot and bring to a boil. Reduce the heat to medium-low and cook until slightly reduced, 10 to 15 minutes. Add the heavy cream, increase the heat to high, and cook until slightly thickened, about 5 minutes. Season with the salt and hog seasoning. Stir in the butter and once it's melted, fold in the tomatoes. Serve warm or at room temperature.

 RODNEY'S PRO TIP
Belly meat from a barbecued whole hog is best. But any combination of roast pork and bacon can work. If your pork is lean, increase the proportion of bacon.

Loaded Potatoes

SERVES 4

WHEN you're smoking meat, there's a lot of heat generated by the coals that's kind of going to waste. It seems a shame to not use as much of that heat as possible. This recipe allows your coals to do double duty—while the meat is cooking on the grill, potatoes or any other hard vegetables (like carrots, turnips, beets, or other root vegetables) can be cooking below the meat right in the coals. It's the equivalent of a one-pan meal for me. Once the potato is roasted, split it open and stuff it with smoked chicken, white barbecue sauce, bacon, and loads of scallions.

This recipe is designed for a heat level appropriate to smoking, which is in the range of 225° to 250°F. If you are grilling over higher heat, or if your coals are burning and not just smoldering, you don't want to put the potatoes in. The temperature will be too hot and the potatoes will burn.

For the potatoes

4 large russet potatoes or sweet potatoes

1 tablespoon extra-virgin olive oil

2 teaspoons Diamond Crystal kosher salt

For the stuffing

3 cups roughly chopped pit-smoked chicken meat (from a little less than ½ Smoked Chicken, page 118)

½ cup Rodney's White Barbecue Sauce (page 214)

¼ cup Crispy Bacon Bits (page 216)

½ cup thinly sliced scallions (3 to 4 scallions), green and white parts

Roast the potatoes: Lightly scrub the potatoes, removing any traces of soil or debris. Dry them well. Rub them all over with the olive oil (this helps keep the skin of the potatoes from cracking). Sprinkle each potato with salt and then wrap each one in foil. Make sure your coals are smoldering and not actively burning and bury the foil-wrapped potatoes in the coals.

Check the potatoes every 30 minutes or so for 1 hour to 1 hour 30 minutes (the total cooking time depends on the heat of the coals and the size of the potatoes). The potatoes are done when the flesh is soft and a knife can be inserted into the center with little resistance.

Stuff the potatoes: Remove the potatoes from the foil and make a slit from end to end, going almost to the bottom of the potato. Fill each potato with the smoked chicken. Spoon the white barbecue sauce on top. Sprinkle the bacon bits and scallions on top and serve.

⚜ RODNEY'S PRO TIP

You can use smoked pork instead of chicken. If you do that, substitute Rodney's Sauce (page 211) for the white barbecue sauce.

Rodney's Reluctant Collard Greens

EVERYBODY else was eating collard greens around me growing up, but I never had the liking for them. It's funny that now they're one of the most popular menu items (aside from the meat!) that we offer.

The very first time I remember tasting collards, they just seemed bitter to me. They hit my tongue and something just said, "No." They were on my plate with white rice and a pork chop. When you're a kid, you eat all your meat, but you don't want to eat your vegetables. So I ate all my pork chop and when I was told to eat my veggies, I cornered off the rice away from the greens and ate that. I left the greens behind. That became the pattern. My mom did all the things you do with kids. She would tell me how good collards were for my health. She would try to make me sit there till I ate them. None of it worked. Finally she just gave up and started making a little pot of sweet peas or field peas or something she knew I would eat.

Funny thing, I didn't have a problem with other greens. Mustard greens? Yes. Turnip greens? Yes. When cabbage was on the menu, I was running to be at the table first. So when I was almost a teenager, I tasted them again. I figured maybe I was wrong before. But I decided that I still didn't like them. There's just something weird about collards that I don't like.

The problem was there were definitely more collards than anything when I was coming up because every garden in Nesmith and in Hemingway had

(recipe continues)

them. So collards are what we got served. Especially on New Year's Day. You had to eat some Hoppin' John and collard greens. That was the tradition for good luck.

When we opened the restaurant in Charleston, Nick said, "You got to have collards on the menu." He said that, along with corn bread, it was one of the go-to sides for barbecue. For most people, those two just naturally go together. I knew he was right. I'm not just cooking for me; I'm cooking for a lot of people who love their collard greens. So I reluctantly agreed.

The whole point of the menu was to try to make it as close as possible to the food I grew up on. When I started working with our culinary director, Paul Yeck, to develop the collards recipe, I tried to re-create the greens according to memory—even though I barely ever tasted them! I told him that my mom always used some of our barbecued pork in the greens. So we did that. Then we decided to try a little bit of the sauce in it, too. That would give it a little sweetness and a little vinegar bite. Both of these things, of course, I like. Since I didn't really want to taste the collards even while we were testing the recipes, I just went off the smell and kept looking for that aroma the greens had when my mother would make them. I would go to the collard pot and inhale to see if we were close to what I remember. I knew that when we had the aroma right, we'd have the greens right.

A couple of years ago, chef Michael Symon came to the restaurant to film us for an episode of his show *Burgers, Brew & 'Que.* I made the mistake of telling him in advance that I didn't like collards. Why did I do that? After that, he just *had* to get me on camera eating those greens. My wife and one of my staff members took out their camera phones. They wanted to capture the look on my face the moment when I put the greens in my mouth. They were having a ball knowing I was sweating just thinking about what I was going to have to do. So I thought for a minute, then I said to myself, "If I'm going to taste these greens I have to have something in my mouth that was going to allow me to chew them and swallow. So I fished around the pot to find the biggest of piece of pork I could and then scooped up some collards with the meat. That gave me the flavor to eat the collards. It was like the meat was the main course with a little bit of collards on the side.

A lot of our customers rave about our collard greens. When they do, I just smile and say thank you.

4 tablespoons unsalted butter

½ medium yellow onion, diced

2 garlic cloves, minced

3 pounds collard greens, washed, tough ends trimmed, leaves stacked, rolled, and cut into 1-inch-wide ribbons

1 smoked ham hock

2½ teaspoons Diamond Crystal kosher salt

1½ tablespoons sugar

2 tablespoons Rodney's Sauce (page 211)

In a large Dutch oven, melt the butter over medium heat. Add the onion and garlic and cook, stirring occasionally, until the onion is translucent, 5 to 10 minutes. Add the collard greens and stir until slightly wilted. If all of the greens don't fit, reduce the heat, cover the pot, and allow the greens to wilt and reduce in volume before adding another handful or two. Repeat as necessary until all the greens are in the pot.

Add the smoked ham hock and 6 cups water. Cover and cook over medium-high heat, stirring occasionally, until the greens are fork-tender, about 1 hour 30 minutes. Stir in the salt, sugar, and Rodney's sauce and serve.

Corn Bread with Honey Butter

YOU have to understand—*Soul Train* on a Saturday was like going to church on Sunday—you just didn't miss it. I'd watch the show at my grandmother's house—she lived in Nesmith, a little way up the road. As a side to *Soul Train*, I'd have my grandmother's corn bread. So when I started working on my menu, there was no doubt in my mind that there would be corn bread on it—and it would be sweet. My grandmother used to make her corn bread using the Jiffy box mix. That was sweet. Then sometimes she'd serve it with Cane Patch syrup on the side, making it even sweeter.

To develop the recipe for the restaurant, we just kept trying different things until that memory would hit of how grandma's corn bread would taste. We added a little more sugar to the corn bread and made it a little more cakey, too. Then we finished it off with honey butter, which is sort of a nod to the way my grandmother sometimes served syrup on the side.

My cousin Larry, better known as Tate, is about twelve years older than me. He came into the restaurant with my mom and his mom, Aunt Fannie. When he bit into that corn bread and he said, "How did you get grandma's corn bread recipe? And his mother, who is older than my mother, said, "Yeah, tastes just like mama's corn bread." That's when I knew for sure we had gotten it right.

There's only one thing missing: a color TV with a bunch of kids sitting in front of it, eating corn bread and watching *Soul Train*.

2 cups cornmeal (preferably fine ground, but medium ground will work)

1½ cups all-purpose flour

⅓ cup sugar

1 teaspoon baking powder

1 teaspoon baking soda

½ teaspoon Diamond Crystal kosher salt

2 large eggs

3 cups buttermilk

1 stick (4 ounces) unsalted butter, melted

Honey Butter (recipe follows), for serving

Preheat the oven to 350°F. Generously coat a 9 × 11-inch baking dish or a 10-inch cast-iron skillet with cooking spray.

In a medium bowl, mix together the cornmeal, flour, sugar, baking powder, baking soda, and salt. In a separate medium bowl, whisk the eggs until well beaten. Whisk in the buttermilk and melted butter until well blended. Slowly pour the buttermilk mixture into the cornmeal mixture and whisk until completely smooth.

Scrape the cornbread batter into the baking dish or skillet and smooth out the top. Transfer to the oven and bake until a cake tester inserted into the center of the corn bread comes out with just a crumb or two attached, about 25 minutes.

Set the corn bread aside to cool slightly before cutting. Serve hot or warm with the honey butter.

HONEY BUTTER

Makes ¾ cup

1 stick (4 ounces) unsalted butter, at room temperature

¼ cup honey

In a medium bowl, beat the honey and butter together with a whisk or electric hand mixer until well combined.

Hushpuppies

SERVES 4 TO 6

I didn't have a lot of hushpuppies growing up. Sometimes my mother would pick up seafood from a take-out spot, and there would be hushpuppies as a side dish. Sometimes I'd eat them; sometimes I wouldn't. Back then, I preferred the ones without onions to the ones with. Times have changed. These days, my hushpuppies have to have onions. They really enhance the flavor and add a little variety to the mouthfeel as you are eating them.

1¾ cups cornmeal (preferably fine ground, but medium ground will work)

1¾ cups all-purpose flour

4½ tablespoons sugar

1¼ teaspoons baking soda

1¼ teaspoons Diamond Crystal kosher salt

1 large egg

1¼ cups buttermilk

2½ tablespoons canola or vegetable oil

¼ cup chopped onion

2 cups vegetable oil, for frying

Honey Butter (page 163), for serving

In a large bowl, combine the cornmeal, flour, sugar, baking soda, and salt. In another bowl, whisk together the egg, buttermilk, canola oil, and onion. Add the buttermilk mixture ingredients to the cornmeal mixture and whisk just until combined.

Pour 3 inches of vegetable oil into a large cast-iron skillet and heat to 350° to 365°F.

Working in batches to not crowd the pan, drop the batter by tablespoons into the oil. Fry until golden brown, 2 to 2½ minutes. Drain on paper towels.

Serve warm with honey butter.

164 • RODNEY SCOTT'S WORLD OF BBQ

Macaroni and Cheese

I remember being in my twenties, driving the church van to Charleston to a church convention or a bishop's gathering or something. The church needed me to drive and my daddy let me off work to do that. We ate at a restaurant called Alice's Fine Cooking. Amazing food. Amazing food! Baked chicken, deviled crab, okra soup—she made it all taste good. But her mac and cheese is what really stands out in my memory.

One day I was walking around my restaurant checking on my guests, and guess who's sitting there. Miss Alice! She said "How you doing? My name is Alice Warren. I used to run a restaurant on King Street years ago."

I sat down.

"You have no idea how many times I've called your name. I've told people about the memories you created for me."

She started telling me about the challenges that had come about and the issues she'd had with her health and so forth. It felt good to sit and reminisce and to know that she was enjoying my food as much as I had enjoyed hers all those years ago.

When we started developing the macaroni and cheese recipe for the restaurant, Nick got a recipe from one of his relatives and made some for me to taste. I was blown away by the flavor. Then they told me the secret ingredient—cream of chicken soup! We like to make all of our stuff in house from scratch, but I figured a little cream of chicken soup in the mac and cheese could be an exception.

One day, an older black lady came in and tasted it. I was walking round checking tables like I do, making sure everything was okay. This lady stopped me and said, "That mac and cheese is good. You use cream of chicken soup." My answer to her was "Maybe."

Busted!

But like the lady said, this mac and cheese is good.

¼ cup Diamond Crystal kosher salt

1 pound large elbow macaroni

1 (10.75-ounce) can condensed cream of chicken soup

½ cup heavy cream

1 cup whole milk

1 stick (4 ounces) unsalted butter

1 pound sharp cheddar cheese, shredded (about 4 cups; see Tip)

1 teaspoon table salt

¼ teaspoon freshly ground black pepper

In a large bowl, set up an ice bath with 4 cups of water and 4 cups of ice cubes. Set aside.

In a soup pot, combine 8 cups water and the Diamond Crystal kosher salt and bring to a boil. Add the macaroni and cook for 4 minutes. Drain the pasta in a colander, then pour it into the ice bath to "shock" it, stopping the cooking process. Drain well.

Preheat the oven to 350°F.

In a small sauce pot, combine the condensed soup, cream, milk, and butter and bring to a simmer over medium heat. Whisk in 3 cups of the cheddar, reserving 1 cup for the topping. Season the mixture with the table salt and pepper and remove from the heat.

In a large bowl, combine the cheese sauce with the drained noodles and mix well. Transfer the noodle mixture to a 2-quart baking dish and top with the reserved cheddar. Transfer to the oven and bake for 20 minutes.

Allow the dish to cool slightly before serving.

 RODNEY'S PRO TIP

Don't use preshredded cheese. It's coated with cornstarch to prevent it from clumping, so you won't get the creamy result you're looking for.

King Street Corn

IT is possible you have seen a man who looks exactly like me in a pickup truck in the drive-up of a fast-food chain ordering more corn on the cob than the average person would eat in one sitting. I'm that dude. So you can imagine what it was like for me to taste the Mexican version of one of my favorite dishes. The first time I had it, I was in California with my business partner, Nick, and our official wearer-of-many-hats, Angie Mosier. When Angie came up with this idea of rolling the corn around cracklins I was over the moon.

1 cup crumbled pork skins

1 cup grated parmesan cheese

8 ears corn, shucked

1 cup Duke's mayonnaise

½ cup minced fresh chives

Mix the crumbled pork skins and the parmesan cheese together in a plate or shallow bowl. On a grill, grill pan, or hot skillet, char the corn. When the corn comes off the grill (or pan), slather each ear with mayonnaise, then roll it in the pork skin mixture. Sprinkle with the minced chives and serve.

BBQ Party Deviled Eggs

MAKES
24 EGG HALVES

I think I was a teenager before I had my first deviled egg. It just wasn't one of those things we did. I've been making up for lost time since then, eating them all the time. I love that combination of the well-seasoned stuffing and the bland egg white. I also like that it's a blank canvas. The stuffing for deviled eggs is really basic, but it can host lots of different topping ideas. I like to use my rib rub in place of the standard paprika garnish for a note of spice. Sometimes I'll sprinkle crumbled pork skins over the top to add some crunch, or add a pickle to each for a classic vinegar punch. Pickled okra sliced into little wheels makes a nice visual, or you can garnish it with slices of your favorite pickle.

12 hard-boiled eggs, peeled

½ cup Duke's mayonnaise

2 teaspoons yellow mustard

¼ teaspoon Diamond Crystal kosher salt

Topping options: Rodney's Rib Rub (page 205), pork skin crumble, pickle pieces

Halve the hard-boiled eggs lengthwise and gently scoop out the yolks into a bowl. Reserve the empty egg whites. Add the mayonnaise, mustard, and salt to the yolks and mash together with the back of a fork until smooth. Using a small spoon, scoop some of the egg mixture back into the whites, making a bit of a mound. Garnish with your chosen topping.

Hoppin' John

SERVES 4 TO 6

THE tradition around here is to eat Hoppin' John and collard greens on January 1 so that you'll have money in the new year: The beans in Hoppin' John represent coins and the collards represent greenbacks. As you know by now, collard greens are not my favorite green, so this was not a ritual I followed too closely. I love Hoppin' John, but I guess during my good years, somebody must have been eating my collards for me. Either that or the cabbage that I love worked as a substitute.

Usually Hoppin' John features black-eyed peas. That's how we used to make it where I'm from. But it's really a dish that started on the coast and on the islands off the coast of South Carolina among the Gullah people. There, they have historically made Hoppin' John with red peas. Glenn Roberts, whose company Anson Mills specializes in growing traditional heirloom foods of the South, puts it this way: "Red peas are never served without rice on the Carolina Sea Islands, and red peas are the dominant legume in the culinary history of the Sea Islands."

Red peas do have a black eye, but they are smaller, redder, and sweeter than their more famous cousins. You should seek them out if you want your Hoppin' John to be historically accurate. But you should also seek them out just because you like good eating. This is history that tastes good.

Note that you need to start this dish the night before so the peas have time to soak.

For the peas

8 ounces Anson Mills Sea Island Red Peas

1 stick (4 ounces) unsalted butter

1 large yellow onion, diced

2 tablespoons chopped garlic (about 6 cloves)

4 ounces shredded barbecued pork (or bacon if no pit-smoked pork is available)

½ teaspoon Hog Seasoning (page 202)

4 cups meat or vegetable stock or water

2 tablespoons Diamond Crystal kosher salt

For the rice

4 tablespoons unsalted butter

½ small yellow onion, diced

1½ cups Anson Mills Carolina Gold Rice, rinsed

1 teaspoon Diamond Crystal kosher salt

For serving

Thinly sliced scallions, for garnish

Rodney's Sauce (page 211)

Corn Bread (page 163)

Make the peas: Soak the peas in water to cover overnight. When ready to cook, drain well.

Preheat the oven to 350°F.

In a medium Dutch oven or ovenproof soup pot, melt the butter over medium heat. Add the onion and garlic and cook until translucent, 10 to 12 minutes. Add the pork and cook for another 3 to 5 minutes. Add the soaked and drained peas, the hog seasoning, and stock.

Transfer to the oven and bake until the peas are tender and creamy, about 1 hour. Remove the pot from the oven, season with salt, and set aside.

Meanwhile, make the rice: In a small saucepan, melt the butter over medium heat. And the onion and cook until it becomes soft and translucent, about 5 minutes. Add the rice, 2½ cups water, and the salt and bring to a boil. Remove from the heat and cover tightly with a lid or foil. Allow the rice to steam for 15 minutes. Fluff the rice with a fork

To serve, place about ½ cup rice in each serving bowl. Ladle 1 cup of hot peas over the rice. Top the Hoppin' John with 1 tablespoon thinly sliced scallions. Serve with Rodney's sauce and corn bread on the side.

172 • RODNEY SCOTT'S WORLD OF BBQ

DESS

Angie Mo's Cracklin' Layer Cake

ALL kids have a favorite flavor of birthday cake. For me, it was always yellow cake with chocolate icing. One time, a FatBack Collective event took place around my birthday. Angie Mosier—friend, baker, photographer, confidante—came up with this Rodney-fied version of a birthday cake for me.

While she was assembling it, she happened to be snacking on some of our pork skins and got a brilliant idea of connecting the salty, umami pork cracklins to the sweet frosting. She ended up decorating the cake with pork skins. It was a big salty-sweet hit with the FatBack Collective. I'm willing to bet it'll be a big hit with your friends, too.

You will need three 9-inch round cake pans to make this cake. If you only have two pans, bake off two layers at the same time, setting the remaining batter aside. Then then bake off the remaining layer.

**Butter and flour,
for greasing the pans**

For the yellow cake

3 cups all-purpose flour

1 teaspoon Diamond Crystal kosher salt

1 teaspoon baking powder

4 large eggs, lightly beaten

1 cup whole milk

1 teaspoon vanilla extract

2 sticks (8 ounces) unsalted butter, at room temperature

2 cups sugar

For the chocolate icing

10 ounces semisweet chocolate, roughly chopped into small pieces

3 sticks (12 ounces) unsalted butter, at room temperature

1 teaspoon Diamond Crystal kosher salt

1 teaspoon vanilla extract

6 cups powdered sugar (about 1½ pounds)

4 to 5 tablespoons whole milk or half-and-half

For assembly

2 cups cracklins (see page 135)

Preheat the oven to 350°F. Grease and flour three 9-inch round cake pans.

Make the yellow cake: In a large bowl, sift together the flour, salt, and baking powder. In a medium bowl, whisk together the eggs, milk, and vanilla.

In a stand mixer with the paddle (or in a bowl with a hand mixer), cream the butter and sugar together on medium speed until fluffy, 1 to 2 minutes. Add about one-third of the flour mixture to the butter mixture and mix on medium speed until just blended. Add half of the milk mixture, mixing until there's no flour visible. Repeat alternating the flour and milk mixtures, ending with the final one-third of the flour mixture, scraping the bottom and sides of the bowl with a spatula as needed. Mix until all the ingredients are well incorporated and there are no visible lumps (do not overmix). Divide the batter evenly into the prepared pans.

(recipe continues)

Bake until a cake tester or toothpick inserted into the center of each pan comes out clean, 25 to 30 minutes. Remove the pans from the oven and allow the cakes to cool in the pans for 5 minutes before flipping them out onto wire cooling racks to cool completely.

Meanwhile, make the chocolate icing: Bring an inch or two of water to a boil in a medium saucepan. Place the chocolate in a heatproof bowl and set the bowl over the saucepan (the bottom of the bowl shouldn't touch the water). Reduce the heat to a simmer and stir the chocolate occasionally until it is completely melted. (This can also be done in a microwave-safe bowl in the microwave by using 15-second blasts and stirring the chocolate after each blast.) Set the melted chocolate aside and allow to cool slightly (but not back to solid).

In a stand mixer with the paddle (or in a large bowl with a hand mixer), cream the butter, salt, and vanilla together on high speed until smooth, scraping the bottom and sides of the bowl as needed. With the mixer on low speed, start adding the powdered sugar gradually, allowing the butter and sugar to cream together before adding more, and stopping the mixer to scrape down the sides as you go. The mixture should look a little dry at this point. With the mixer running, slowly pour in the melted chocolate, scraping down the sides well to incorporate the chocolate completely. Start adding the milk 1 tablespoon at a time and beating on medium-high speed until you get a creamy texture that still has enough body to frost the cake without it running off. Be careful not to add too much milk—just add it 1 tablespoon at a time—because it is difficult to get the proper texture back once too much liquid is added. The icing can be made ahead and refrigerated. When you are ready to use it, you will have to remove it from the refrigerator, let it come back to room temperature, and beat it again with the mixer.

Assemble the cake: Place one of the cooled cake layers on a cake plate or cardboard cake round. Spread some icing on the top of the first round and then top with another cake layer. Spread more icing on the top of that layer and then add the final layer of cake on top. Frost the top and sides of the cake with the remaining icing and create some texture by using your icing spatula to swirl the frosting.

Surround the bottom border of the cake with cracklins and place some of the rinds on the top. (Alternatively, the pork rinds can be crushed up and sprinkled on top of the cake or pressed into the sides.)

Apple Hand Pies

THE closest thing I had to hand pies made from scratch when was a kid was the apple turnover at Hardee's. I wasn't even a big fan of those until one day in about 1989, I was hanging with my cousin Curly and we both ordered the turnovers and strawberry milkshakes. I fell in love with them that day. I got to the point where I ate two turnovers and a strawberry milkshake every morning for breakfast. Thank goodness my metabolism was in the left lane then, speeding along the highway of life! This recipe takes everything I loved about fried pies from fast-food restaurants—flaky crust, sweet fruit with a little lemon juice kick—and makes it much, much better. I adapted it from my friend Lisa Marie Donovan. She used to be the pastry chef at Husk in Nashville. When it comes to Southern pastries, she's dah bomb!

Note that the hand-pie dough needs to chill for 3 hours before rolling. While the dough is in the fridge, you can bake and chill the apples, too.

For the hand-pie dough

3 sticks (12 ounces) cold unsalted butter, cut into 1-inch pieces

Ice

2⅓ cups all-purpose flour

2¼ teaspoons Diamond Crystal kosher salt

For the filling

4 to 5 apples (I like a mix of Honeycrisp and Granny Smith), cored and diced into 1-inch chunks (about 5 cups)

⅓ cup apple juice

1 teaspoon fresh lemon juice

¼ cup granulated sugar

¼ cup packed dark brown sugar

2 teaspoons cornstarch

1 teaspoon Diamond Crystal kosher salt

¼ teaspoon vanilla bean paste or vanilla extract

Pinch of ground cinnamon

For baking

1 large egg

Flour, for the work surface

Granulated sugar

Make the hand pie dough: Place the cubed butter in a bowl and in the refrigerator while you prepare the dry ingredients. Fill a tall glass with ice and add at least ½ cup water.

In a large bowl, whisk together the flour and salt. Working quickly to keep the butter as cold as possible, toss the butter in the flour mixture and then use your hands and fingers to work the butter pieces into the flour. Continue until all the butter has been thoroughly incorporated and the butter pieces are the size of small peas.

Measure out ½ cup of the ice water and drizzle 3 tablespoons of it into the flour. Using your hands as paddles (do NOT knead or squeeze), simply toss and combine until the flour has absorbed the water. Repeat this process, adding the water 1 tablespoon at a time until the dough starts to form a ball. Once the dough comes together and feels supple and tacky (but not sticky), knead it three or four quick times to pull it all together. Divide the dough into two equal parts and flatten each into 5-inch-diameter discs. Wrap each portion tightly in plastic wrap and refrigerate for at least 3 hours or overnight.

Preheat the oven to 400°F.

Make the filling: In a large bowl, toss together the apples, apple juice, and lemon juice. In another bowl, whisk together the granulated sugar, brown sugar, cornstarch, and salt. Add the sugar mixture to the apples and toss. Add the vanilla and cinnamon and mix thoroughly.

Pour the apples into an 8 × 8-inch baking pan. Transfer to the oven and bake for about 20 minutes. Stir the apple mixture to ensure that all the pieces are evenly cooked. Then continue to cook until the apples are softened, but still a little firm at the center, about an additional 25 minutes. Remove the apple mixture from the oven and set aside to cool for 30 minutes before refrigerating for at least 2 hours (or overnight) before filling and forming pies.

(recipe continues)

Shape and bake the hand pies: Line 2 baking sheets with parchment paper. In a small bowl, beat the egg with 1 tablespoon water and set the egg wash aside.

Unwrap the pie dough discs and transfer them to a lightly floured surface and sprinkle a little flour over the dough. Roll each disc of dough until it is ¼ inch thick. Using a 6-inch round cookie cutter or an upturned soup bowl, cut out 12 rounds. Arrange the pastry rounds on parchment-lined baking sheets.

Brush the edges of each round with the egg wash. Spoon ¼ cup chilled apple filling onto the center of each dough round. For each pie, fold the dough up and over the filling to make a half-moon and press lightly to seal the edges. Brush the tops of all of the pies with egg wash and sprinkle each pie with a pinch of sugar.

Refrigerate the pies, uncovered, until chilled, at least 15 minutes or up to a few hours.

Preheat the oven to 375°F.

Bake the hand pies until they are golden brown, 28 to 32 minutes. Remove from the oven and allow to cool for as long as you can stand to wait. Eat warm or at room temperature. The pies can last a couple of days unrefrigerated and up to 5 days in the refrigerator

Banana Pudding | SERVES 4 TO 6

ALMOST every Sunday my mother made banana pudding. She didn't finish hers off with cookie crumbs the way we do at the restaurant, because in the old days all the broken cookie pieces came straight to me. At first that was why I loved it when my mother made banana pudding. Later, I learned to love the pudding itself. Like a lot of women who had too much work and too little time to do it in, my mother got to the point where she enjoyed the ease of using instant pudding in her recipe sometimes. So when we got ready to create a version of this recipe for the restaurant, I called on my friend Lisa Marie Donovan to help out. She really knows her way around the Southern dessert table.

For the vanilla pudding

2 cups whole milk

2 teaspoons vanilla paste (Nielsen-Massey Madagascar Bourbon is the best, but vanilla extract works just fine)

¾ cup sugar

¼ cup all-purpose flour

1 teaspoon Diamond Crystal kosher salt

1 large egg

4 large egg yolks

1 cup heavy cream

For the vanilla Chantilly cream

2 cups heavy cream

½ cup powdered sugar

½ teaspoon vanilla extract

For the banana pudding

1 box Nilla wafers (roughly 100 cookies; see Tip)

3 ripe bananas, sliced to your liking (thick cut is my favorite)

Make the vanilla pudding: In a medium saucepan, combine the milk and vanilla paste and whisk over medium heat, being careful not to let the milk boil.

In a bowl, make a slurry by whisking together the sugar, flour, salt, whole egg, and egg yolks. Whisk the cream into the egg slurry. Temper the slurry with a few tablespoons of hot milk so the slurry becomes loose enough to pour. Slowly whisk the slurry mixture into the hot milk in the saucepan. Cook this mixture over medium-low heat, stirring constantly so that you don't scorch the bottom, until it thickens, 10 to 15 minutes. It should coat the back of a wooden spoon. Once thickened, remove from the heat and strain through a sieve into a bowl to remove any lumps. The texture should be smooth.

Make the Chantilly cream: In a stand mixer with the whisk (or in a large bowl with an electric mixer), beat the cream, powdered sugar, and vanilla on medium speed until you have stiff peaks (meaning when you remove the whisk from the cream, the whipped cream makes a point that stands straight up).

Assemble the banana pudding: Allow the strained vanilla pudding to come to room temperature. Arrange a layer of the whole Nilla wafers over the bottom of an 8 × 8-inch baking pan. Spread the vanilla pudding on top of the cookies, making the layer as even as you can. Add the sliced bananas over the pudding. Spread the whipped cream over the bananas and top it all off with the crumbled vanilla wafers. Refrigerate for at least an hour before serving. Covered tightly with foil or plastic wrap, the banana pudding will keep up to 4 days in the refrigerator.

 RODNEY'S PRO TIP

At the restaurant, our banana pudding only has one layer of whole vanilla wafers. If you want to create multiple layers, kind of like an English trifle, you might need more cookies.

Roscoe's Blueberry Cornmeal Pound Cake

SERVES 10 TO 12

WHY we had blueberries hanging around the restaurant I do not recall. Why Roscoe decided to put them in cornbread, I can only answer, "That's Roscoe. Always playing with his food." Roscoe comes from the lineage of Dreamland Bar-B-Que people, and he has also cooked at some outstanding white-tablecloth restaurants around the country. So he has his foot in two camps: the traditional Southern-cooking camp and the fancy fine-dining camp. When he plays around in the kitchen, he always produces something delicious. Of course, when I asked him to write up the recipe for the book, he had to go and dress it up with the bourbon Chantilly cream. Roscoe!

For the pound cake

Butter, for greasing the skillet

2 cups finely ground cornmeal

1½ cups all-purpose flour

1½ cups sugar

1 teaspoon baking soda

1 teaspoon baking powder

½ teaspoon Diamond Crystal kosher salt

3 cups buttermilk

10 tablespoons unsalted butter, melted

3 large eggs

1 tablespoon vanilla extract

2 cups blueberries

For the macerated berries

4 cups blueberries

¼ cup sugar

2 tablespoons grated lemon zest

1 tablespoon fresh lemon juice

Pinch of salt

For the bourbon Chantilly cream

2 cups heavy cream

½ cup powdered sugar

1 tablespoon bourbon

Preheat the oven to 350°F. Grease a 10-inch cast-iron skillet with some butter and set aside.

Make the pound cake: In a large bowl, combine the cornmeal, flour, sugar, baking soda, baking powder, and salt. In a medium bowl, combine the buttermilk, melted butter, eggs, and vanilla. Add the buttermilk mixture to the cornmeal mixture and stir them together. Don't work the mixture too much or the cake will become tough and not rise as much.

Pour the batter into the prepared skillet, spreading it out evenly. Sprinkle the blueberries over the batter. Bake the corn bread until a cake tester inserted into the center comes out clean, about 45 minutes. Set aside to cool slightly.

Macerate the berries: Place the berries in a medium bowl. Add the sugar, lemon zest, lemon juice, and salt. Toss all the ingredients until the blueberries are coated completely. The sugar and salt will draw out the juices from the blueberries. Cover the bowl and leave it at room temperature for 2 hours, then refrigerate. Stored in an airtight container, they will keep in the refrigerator for up to 5 days.

Make the Chantilly cream: In a stand mixer with the whisk attachment (or in a large bowl with a hand mixer), whip the cream, powdered sugar, and bourbon on medium speed until you have stiff peaks (meaning when you remove the whisk from the cream, the whipped cream makes a point that stands straight up).

To serve, cut the cake into squares or wedges and top with the macerated berries and bourbon Chantilly cream.

COCKT

My parents used to say, "I don't have to drink to have a good time." And they were true to their word. I don't ever remember seeing either one of them with a drink.

I had a little different philosophy. "If I can feel this good without drinking, imagine what a little liquor will do." I have to hand it to them, though, my parents didn't mind if other people had a sip or three. At the Easter picnics we would have in Hemingway, there was always a cooler for the drinkers among the cousins and the aunts and uncles. There was beer, course, and also Cask & Cream, Crown Royal, Courvoisier, gin, and the like. Back in the day, when I went out, I was mostly a bourbon man with some occasional rum drinks thrown into the mix. My travels have also widened my taste in drinks. When I was in Uruguay I remember having a cocktail of local rum, sugar, and fruit juice. It didn't seem like such a big deal then, but the taste of that drink has lingered with me years later. I told that to Nicholas, my business partner's son. He just said, "I got you."

So he came up with The Punch-n the Carolinas, a tribute to that great Uruguayan cocktail. In fact, Nicholas is the man most responsible for designing the drinks at the restaurants. He works hard and he likes to party. So assigning him the "work" of designing cocktails seemed like a no-brainer. I wasn't with him for the research and development, which is probably a good thing.

We use our barbecue sauce as elements in two of these cocktails. That's all about taking the flavors that we have been refining for years and translating them into a new context. The sweet and sour, yin and yang that make for a good, balanced cocktail is the same push-pull flavor sensation I try to achieve in my barbecue. So these cocktails complement the barbecue in that way. I think they also whet the appetite for the meat.

🔥 **RODNEY'S PRO TIP**
For all cocktails, fresh juice is recommended, but if you're on the go, my recommendation would be to use Santa Cruz Organic juices.

Pee Dee Old-Fashioned

MAKES 1 COCKTAIL

THE Pee Dee in the title doesn't mean that this cocktail is something that people in my hometown drink. Instead it's playing with the flavors that people in the Pee Dee region of South Carolina enjoy and then presenting them in a new way. Remember, nothing is more old-fashioned than change.

3 dashes Angostura bitters

¼ ounce BBQ Brown Sugar Syrup (recipe follows)

½ ounce Cynar 70 Proof Amaro

1½ ounces rye whiskey (preferably High Wire Distilling Co.)

1 long strip orange peel

1 long strip lemon peel

In a mixing glass, combine the bitters, BBQ syrup, Cynar, and rye. Stir and then pour into a double old-fashioned glass. Add an ice cube (I like the big 2-inch cubes).

Take the strip of orange peel and squeeze and twist the strip directly over the glass to release the volatile oils into the cocktail. Then rub the peel around the rim of the glass before adding it to the cocktail. Repeat with the lemon peel and serve.

BBQ BROWN SUGAR SYRUP

Makes about ¾ cup

¼ cup Rodney's Sauce (page 211)

¾ cup packed light brown sugar

In a small saucepan, warm Rodney's sauce over medium-low heat to a near simmer. Add the brown sugar and stir until it is dissolved. Once the sugar is dissolved, remove the syrup from the heat and allow to cool completely before using. Store in an airtight container. It will keep refrigerated for up to 1 month.

Punch-n the Carolinas

MAKES
16 COCKTAILS

VERY seldom do you hear of somebody making barbecue for one person. You might do that if you're practicing your 'que skills, but usually if you go through the trouble of firing up the grill, you invite friends and family members. If you've got all those people coming over, it's helpful to have a cocktail that you can make in advance for a large group. Sweet tea is the unofficial drink of the South. And nothing says sweet tea like this Punch-n the Carolinas.

2 cups simple syrup (see Box)

1½ cups fresh lemon juice (preferably from Meyer lemons)

Generous 3 cups unsweetened black tea

1 cup amaro (preferably High Wire Distilling Southern Amaro Liqueur)

1 cup dark rum (preferably Plantation O.F.T.D. Rum)

3 cups rye whiskey (preferably Old Forester 100 Proof Rye)

2 cups thinly sliced lemon wheels

Fresh mint, for garnish

In a pitcher, combine the simple syrup, lemon juice, tea, amaro, rum, and whiskey. Stir to combine and refrigerate until well chilled. To serve, place a lemon wheel on the rim of a rocks glass and place a large ice cube in the glass. Pour the punch into the glass, and garnish with fresh mint.

Simple syrup is just that: simple. Equal parts water and sugar cooked into a syrup. To make it, in a saucepan, bring the water to a boil and add the sugar. Stir until the sugar is dissolved. Turn off the heat and set aside to cool. Once the syrup is at room temperature, refrigerate until thoroughly chilled. Simple syrup can be refrigerated for up to 3 weeks. To get the 2 cups simple syrup needed for the punch on this page, make the syrup with 1⅓ cups water and 1⅓ cups sugar.

Red Pickup

WHEN I have an important call and I don't want to be distracted by customers or staff, I walk out of the restaurant and take the call in my red pickup. When I have to check on the progress of our restaurants in Birmingham and Atlanta, I'd rather hop in my red pickup than hop on a plane. When I need to clear my head, I jump into my red pickup, play my music, and take a drive to nowhere in particular. This is my red pickup in a glass.

¾ ounce fresh lime juice

½ ounce cranberry juice

½ ounce Ruby Red grapefruit juice

¾ ounce simple syrup (see Box, page 193)

¼ ounce Campari

¼ ounce cachaça (preferably Avuá Prata)

½ ounce Lillet Blanc

1¼ ounces gin (preferably Hat Trick Botanical Gin)

Crushed ice (see Tip)

Ice cubes

Lime wheel, for garnish

In a cocktail shaker, combine the lime juice, cranberry juice, grapefruit juice, simple syrup, Campari, cachaça, Lillet, and gin. Sprinkle a small handful of crushed ice into the shaker, cover, and shake vigorously for 10 to 15 seconds. Strain into a tall ice-filled glass. Garnish with a lime wheel on the rim of the glass.

RODNEY'S PRO TIP
To make crushed ice, place ice cubes in a plastic bag and smash it with a heavy-bottomed pot.

Hemingway Golden Gate

FOR several years I've cooked at the annual La Cocina San Francisco Street Food Festival. That organization helps low-income entrepreneurs in food businesses grow and formalize their enterprises. One year Angie Mosier, one of my partners in culinary crime, made a taco with some of my barbecue and a tortilla that had been made just a few feet from where we were standing. Alma Rodriguez, the chef and owner of Mixiote in San Francisco, made it by hand. When I tasted that tortilla and my pork, it was like tasting my own cooking for the first time. The marriage of the honey-vinegar barbecue sauce and tequila in this drink is like the marriage of flavors I had at that festival in San Francisco.

Ice

¾ ounce fresh lemon juice

¾ ounce Honey-Barbecue Sauce Syrup (recipe follows)

2 ounces tequila (preferably Tapatio Blanco 110)

Dehydrated lemon wheel, for garnish (see Tip)

In an ice-filled cocktail shaker, combine the lemon juice, barbecue sauce syrup, and tequila. Cover and shake vigorously for 10 to 15 seconds. Strain (optional) into a chilled glass (a double old-fashioned glass is nice) and garnish with a dehydrated lemon wheel.

🌢 **RODNEY'S PRO TIP**

Dehydrating lemon wheels is easy and makes this cocktail a little more special. To do so, slice a lemon very thinly into wheels. Place them on a baking sheet and bake at 225°F for 2 hours or until dry and crisp.

HONEY-BARBECUE SAUCE SYRUP

Makes enough for 16 cocktails

½ cup Rodney's Sauce (page 211)

1 cup local honey

In a small saucepan, heat the Rodney's sauce and honey over medium heat until the honey melts into the sauce. Remove from the heat and cool completely. Refrigerate in an airtight container for up to 2 weeks if not using immediately.

"OTHER"   WHITE SA   KATHY'S SAU

THE P

When it was just me and a couple of other guys cooking in Hemingway every day, we didn't necessarily need to mix our rubs and spices in bulk. We knew what seasonings we were going to use and we knew from experience what everything was supposed to taste like. I'm sure it wasn't exactly the same from week to week, hog to hog. But since the same people were doing it, using the same technique every time, we were damn close.

The plan for Rodney Scott's Whole Hog BBQ was to have a lot of people in a lot of locations cooking the food and having it taste the same in every place every time. That was the original reason to develop the pantry recipes. Since then, I've learned that there are a lot of other reasons to take the time to mix your spices and sauces in advance.

The most obvious reason is convenience. You can just pull what you need right off the shelf. But just as we look for consistency in our restaurants, home cooks need to have consistency in their dishes as well. Who out there hasn't had this experience: You cook a great meal when nobody is there to eat it but you. Then you try to replicate that for company and it's just not the same. A good pantry can help you cook it the same every time.

I've also learned that different brands of spices have different flavors and concentra-tion levels. Salt X might be saltier than Salt Y and I'm not just talking about kosher salt versus table salt. I'm talking about different brands of the same style of salt. As you learn the ingredients in your pantry, you can adjust and accommodate differences like that. We use Diamond Crystal Kosher salt because we like the texture and it's a little less salty than Morton's kosher salt, the other popular brand. You can always add more salt; you can't take salt away.

I know some people think that doing all this stuff in advance limits your creativity. It's actually the opposite. If you know how your ingredients will taste, it's easier to improvise and come up with variations. The pantry in the kitchen is like the bass and the drums in a band. Once you got that firm foundation under you, there's no limit to what you can do.

Hog Seasoning

WHEN I was cooking at Scott's Pit Cook B.B.Q. in Hemingway, we used to sprinkle the seasonings on the hogs one at a time rather than mixing them all together and sprinkling them on at once. That meant you had to have a good feel for the amounts of salt and pepper you wanted to add. There's no way to get a consistent product if you're relying on several different pitmasters to use the right amount of seasoning every time. It took a few tries to get these proportions right. But now that we have it down, it's foolproof.

We use this rub for the whole hogs. For most other dishes, we use the rib rub. But there's no reason not to use this on pork shoulder or pork chops or even chicken, for that matter.

½ cup table salt

⅓ cup cayenne pepper

⅓ cup MSG (Jesus's Tears, see page 208)

⅓ cup red pepper flakes

¼ cup freshly ground black pepper

Mix all of the ingredients and place them in an airtight container. Cover and store in a cool dry place until ready to use.

A Note on Storage

In the restaurants, we don't worry about "use by" dates. We use things up so fast that nothing sits around long enough to lose its freshness. But when you're writing a cookbook you have to give instructions for how to store things and how long they will last. When I started doing this I called Paul, our culinary director, and suggested to him that we write that the sauces will last for three weeks if stored properly. He put it in perspective in a way I hadn't thought of. "Do you throw away your ketchup after three weeks?"

I know. Most commercial condiments and dressings are so loaded with preservatives that you could probably keep them forever. These sauces don't have all that stuff in them, but they are still pretty shelf-stable. Vinegar, salt, sugar—all these things are used to preserve foods. Think about pickles, salt cod, and fruit preserves. All of those things were invented so that you could take something when you had a lot of it and keep it for when you didn't have so much.

These storage instructions err on the side of being safe, but you should also feel free to use your common sense. If we say the sauce is good for three weeks, that doesn't mean you have to throw it out after twenty-two days. Smell it. Taste it. And keep it as long as you think it's safe and tasty.

Rib Rub

FOR years, I seasoned my ribs on the pit just like I seasoned my hogs. But when we opened in Charleston, I rethought the rib seasoning and developed this rub. The main difference between the rib rub and the hog seasoning is the light brown sugar. It's not much sweetness. It's just enough and that sweet-savory contrast is magical for me. Soon, it was the go-to seasoning for almost half the menu. For most of our dishes, we use the rib rub.

½ cup Diamond Crystal kosher salt

¼ cup Jesus's Tears (aka MSG, see page 208)

¼ cup freshly ground black pepper

¼ cup paprika

¼ cup chili powder

¼ cup packed light brown sugar

2 tablespoons garlic powder

2 tablespoons onion powder

1 teaspoon cayenne pepper

Mix all of the ingredients and place them in an airtight container. Cover and store in a cool dry place until ready to use.

GARLIC
POWDER

JESUS'S
TEARS

ONION
POWDER

KOSHER
SALT

CAYENNE
PEPPER

BROWN SUGAR

CHILI POWDER

PAPRIKA

BLACK PEPPER

Jesus's Tears

Yes, there is MSG in our food.

MSG is monosodium glutamate and a lot of people have concerns about it these days. Some people even say that they are allergic to it. I respect that, and I'm also upfront about the fact that we use it.

We use MSG because it really does enhance the flavor of food. It's kind of like salt. Just like putting a little salt on something can wake up all the other flavors, MSG can do the same thing. But you still have to do the work to get the flavor of the food. Just like you can't throw a bunch of salt on something and expect it to taste good, you can't just sprinkle MSG like some kind of cure-all for bad food.

The first time I saw MSG being used, my dad was sprinkling it on a hog. His uncle, the man who taught him how to cook a hog, used to use it, too. So it's not something that just popped up for us. We've been using it for generations. And whether you know it or not, you've probably been eating it for generations, too. Look at the ingredient list on the packages of Nacho Cheese Doritos, Fritos Honey BBQ Flavor Twists, Ruffles Sour Cream & Onion potato chips, Hidden Valley Ranch dressing, and Campbell's Homestyle Chicken Noodle Soup. And even though the fast-food chains don't put out their ingredient lists, there are lots of articles saying that MSG is an ingredient in those fast-food fried chicken sandwiches people are so crazy about.

Because people have concerns about it, I did some research. One of the things I found out was that in some of the studies that concluded MSG was bad for you, they gave people a lot of it, much more than you would get in a regular serving of food. I get it. They are trying to imitate what would happen if you ate a lot of it over a long period of time. But just like with salt, if you get too much of it all at once, it can cause you problems. MSG actually has about one-third less sodium than salt—who knows, at least for some people it's probably even safer than salt is.

I have four stories that kind of illustrate my relationship with MSG.

I was in the restaurant one day, talking to a lady. She told me that she was on a strict diet and only ate certain things. One of the things she didn't eat was MSG. But she had already eaten our food. I was like "Whoa! Do you have an allergy or something, because we use MSG?" She said it didn't make her sick and that was that.

Another time I was cooking with a chef at a very fancy restaurant out of town. I realized that I had forgotten to bring the MSG. I asked the chef where the nearest restaurant supply store was. He asked me what I needed; he might have it. I told him I needed some MSG. "You can't ever tell anybody that this was in my business," he told me. And he went to the kitchen and got what I needed.

Chef David Chang tasted my pork and I was standing right there. He said "Damn, Rodney. You're Asian!" He could taste the MSG. He knew from the beginning it was in there. He's been one of the main people talking about how MSG has gotten a bum rap in the United States. He says at his restaurants, they don't add MSG, but they use a lot of ingredients that naturally contain glutamate like soy sauce, dried mushrooms, and country ham. Americans associate glutamate with Asian food. There's even a term, Chinese Restaurant Syndrome to describe the sick feeling some people say they get when they eat MSG. But a lot of foods that aren't Asian, like parmesan cheese and Vegemite, also contain a lot of glutamate. MSG is just manufactured glutamate.

One day Nick and I were seasoning some meat and his son Nicholas walked up and asked, "What's that?"

Nick just told him. "It's MSG."

"Shhh!" Nicholas told him. "Don't say that out loud!" Maybe because he was younger he was more sensitive to what people were saying about it. But the next time we were all cooking together and we broke out the MSG he said. "That's Jesus's Tears. It makes everything better."

So from that day on, we called it Jesus's Tears. I use it in my Hog Seasoning (page 202) as well as in my Rib Rub (page 205) and catfish fry. If it really makes you worried, you can leave it out—but know that the resulting food won't be quite like mine.

Rodney's Sauce

BACK in Hemingway we used to make barbecue sauce right next to the pit. The pots we used were too big to really fit on a kitchen stove, plus it was more efficient to use hot coals from the pit as our heat source. We'd put a piece of roofing tin down on the floor and then set some hot coals on top of that, and then we would put the pot right on top of the hot coals. When I was a kid, it was mostly men making the sauce—but I was always the designated stirrer.

You can still do it that way if you want to do all the cooking outside, but these days at the restaurant, we make sauce on the stove.

The two main ingredients are vinegar and pepper, so you have to balance them right. You don't want the vinegar to be overwhelming. Distilled white vinegar has less acid than other white vinegars, so it helps keep the bite in balance. Also, heating the vinegar takes away some of its sharpness.

When it comes to the pepper, you want a little spice, but you don't want it so overwhelming that you can't take it. The goal is to get an immediate heat that goes away just as fast as it started. If it lingers too long, you added too much pepper. You know you have it right when you taste a few drops of the finished sauce and, after you taste it, your mouth forms a kiss.

If you are cooking a whole hog, you'll need a gallon of sauce. But if you're using it for any of the other recipes, you can make only half a gallon.

1 gallon distilled white vinegar

1 lemon, thinly sliced

½ cup ground black pepper

⅓ cup cayenne pepper

1¼ tablespoons red pepper flakes

2 cups sugar

In a small stockpot, warm the vinegar over medium-high heat. After about 5 minutes, when the vinegar reaches 150°F on an instant-read thermometer, just before it starts to simmer, add the lemon slices and continue to cook until the lemon peels begin to soften and wilt, about 10 minutes more.

Whisk in the black pepper, cayenne, pepper flakes, and sugar. Continue to cook over medium-high heat until the sugar is completely dissolved and the sauce reaches 190°F, about 10 minutes. Remove from the heat and allow to completely cool before using. Once the lemon is removed, the sauce can be refrigerated in an airtight container for up to 8 weeks.

The Other Sauce

WHEN Nick and I started talking about opening Rodney Scott's BBQ, he said, "I'll guide you through this whole operation, and you'll be happy with the results. But we need to talk about sauce. You need another one that isn't so spicy, and I have one in mind." He asked me if I had a problem with that, and I told him no.

Then he said, "If we call your sauce Rodney's Sauce, what are we going to call the other sauce?" I said, "The Other Sauce."

The name resonated with me because when I was a teenager there were two places in town to hang out at. Yank's and The Other Place. (Yes, it was really called that.) Mostly white kids used to hang out at Yank's, but every now and then my friends and I would go there because they sold burgers and fries and food like that. We didn't really go to The Other Place because it was a bar and we were all under age. But that name stuck with me. It was simple, memorable, and kind of made you think, "How can you just name something 'The Other Place' unless you first had somewhere called 'The Place'?"

So while there will always be "the sauce," my Rodney's Sauce made with white vinegar and cayenne pepper, this is The Other Sauce, made with apple cider vinegar and ketchup. It's a little thicker and a bit sweeter.

1 cup apple cider vinegar

1 cup ketchup

1 cup Worcestershire sauce

½ cup hot sauce (preferably Texas Pete)

¼ cup packed dark brown sugar

1 tablespoon chili powder

1 tablespoon Diamond Crystal kosher salt

1½ teaspoons freshly ground black pepper

½ teaspoon mustard powder

1 teaspoon cayenne pepper

In a medium saucepan, combine the vinegar, ketchup, Worcestershire sauce, hot sauce, brown sugar, chili powder, salt, pepper, mustard powder, and cayenne pepper. Cook over medium heat for about 10 minutes, stirring frequently to keep the sauce from sticking to the bottom of the pan. Allow the sauce to cool at room temperature. Store in an airtight container in the refrigerator until ready to use. It will keep for up to 3 weeks.

Rodney's White Barbecue Sauce

MAKES 3½ CUPS

I learned about white sauce when I was cooking with the FatBack Collective at the Memphis in May World Championship Barbecue Cooking Contest. Walking around, I would see people put it on their barbecued chicken. Then I tasted it and I was a convert. Compared to what I grew up on, white barbecue sauce opened up a whole new world of flavor. It's mellow. It complements the flavor of the meat without overpowering the seasoning you already have. When I tasted it on some smoked chicken or turkey, I was like, "Where have you been all my life?" So when we started talking about expanding the restaurant to Birmingham, we decided that white sauce would definitely be on the menu. Alabama is, after all, the home of white barbecue sauce. Now we serve it at all our restaurants.

2 cups ranch dressing (preferably Hidden Valley)

1 cup Duke's mayonnaise

½ cup distilled white vinegar

2 tablespoons fresh lemon juice

1 teaspoon Diamond Crystal kosher salt

1 teaspoon freshly ground black pepper

1 teaspoon cayenne pepper

In a large bowl, whisk together the ranch dressing, mayo, vinegar, lemon juice, salt, black pepper, and cayenne until everything is fully incorporated. Store in the refrigerator in a sealed container up to 3 weeks.

Kathy's Sweet Sauce

MAKES 2½ CUPS

I grew up in a world of vinegar-based barbecue sauce, but I understand that for a lot of folks, the definition of barbecue sauce is sweet and tomato-based. That's what they sell in the supermarket. That's the flavor of the barbecue dipping sauce you get with your chicken tenders. I thought we wouldn't have to go that route, but I was wrong. The point was driven home when a friend of Nick's brought his wife in to try our barbecue. Her name was Kathy. "I love everything, but I want a sweeter sauce," she said. Next thing I know, Nick had concocted something, put it in a bottle, put a masking tape label on it, dubbing it "Kathy's Sauce," and stuck it in front of her. One advantage of having several different sauces available is the customers can mix and match them. They can use Rodney's White Barbecue Sauce (opposite) on the barbecued chicken, Rodney's Sauce (page 211) on the greens, Kathy's Sauce on the ribs, and whatever other combinations they can dream up on everything else.

2 cups ketchup

½ cup apple cider vinegar

4½ tablespoons granulated sugar

2 tablespoons plus 1 teaspoon brown sugar

1 tablespoon hot sauce (preferably Texas Pete)

1½ teaspoons freshly ground black pepper

1 teaspoon Diamond Crystal kosher salt

1⅛ teaspoons mustard powder

1⅛ teaspoons red pepper flakes

½ teaspoon chili powder

In a medium saucepan, combine the ketchup, vinegar, both sugars, the hot sauce, black pepper, salt, mustard powder, pepper flakes, and chili powder. Cook over medium heat, stirring frequently to prevent the sauce from sticking to the bottom of the pan, until the sugars are melted and the sauce is smooth, about 10 minutes. Allow the sauce to cool at room temperature and refrigerate in an airtight container for up to 3 weeks.

Crispy Bacon Bits

MAKES ¾ CUP
TO 1 CUP
OF BACON BITS

THERE are not many things that aren't improved by adding some bacon bits—soups, salads, cooked vegetables. I'm only using it in a few recipes here—but I'm sure you can find plenty more.

½ pound thick sliced,
smoked bacon, about
6 strips

In a large, 12-inch cast-iron skillet or nonstick frying pan, lay the bacon in a single layer. Turn the heat to medium-low and allow the bacon to cook slowly for about 6 minutes, until the bacon is mostly cooked and slightly rendered on one side. Turn the strips of bacon over and continue to cook for an additional 4 minutes or until the bacon is golden brown and crisp on all sides.

Remove the bacon from the pan and place onto a paper towel–lined plate, allowing the paper towel to absorb as much of the bacon fat as possible. Place the bacon on a cutting board and, using a chef's knife, chop the bacon into ¼-inch bits. Use immediately as a garnish, or place in a nonreactive container with a lid and store in the refrigerator until ready to use.

ACKNOWLEDGMENTS

I owe the success of Rodney Scott's Whole Hog BBQ to the team that I've been able to assemble. They have deep insights, deep experience, and a total dedication to making us the best we can be. You've read a lot about Nick Pihakis in this book. He had the vision and expertise to help me take what we were doing in Hemingway and present it to the world. There are other people on the Rodney Scott's Whole Hog BBQ team whose names you won't read as often, but whose contributions to the team make us who we are.

I'm older than Paul Yeck, but I still look up to him. First time I met him at Little Donkey, the Pihakis Restaurant Group's Mexican restaurant, he and Nick's son, Nicholas, were all fun and games. But when it got down to taking care of business the next day, he was still upbeat, but he was also focused. He's from Oxford, Mississippi, but he got his culinary training at the French Culinary Institute in New York before working in Washington, DC, with chef José Andrés and then in Birmingham with chef Frank Stitt. He's the executive chef and chief operating officer for the whole Pihakis Restaurant Group. (But we both know that Rodney Scott's is his favorite!) He knows how to standardize recipes so that even the new cooks can follow them. And he knows how to keep his cool, even when there are problems in the kitchen. He's a rock.

Roscoe Hall is a triple threat—barbecue, fine dining, and visual arts. He is the grandson of John Bishop, the founder of Dreamland Bar-

B-Que. But he was too restless to stay in the family business. He got a degree in photography and graphic design from San Diego State University and then got a masters of fine arts in art history at the Savannah College of Art and Design. He describes himself as a punk rock kid who figured out that cooking in restaurants was a way to live in different places and keep a job. In Birmingham, he worked at Frank Stitt's Bottega Cafe. Then he worked for three years at Chez Panisse in Berkeley, and at David Chang's Momofuku Ssäm Bar in New York. I would think that after all those years doing fine dining, he'd want to keep doing it. But he told me that one of the things he really loves about working in our restaurant is making sure the food tastes exactly the same day in and day out. He says that's harder than coming up with a new menu of specials every day and I take him at his word.

You might think Nicholas Pihakis got his job because he's the son of the company founder. When you're out drinking with him late at night, there's nothing about this behavior that would indicate otherwise. But come work time, he works. He asks good questions. He makes good decisions and proves time and time again that he knows this business inside and out. From our first conversation, I never doubted how much of an asset he was, and he keeps proving me right in more ways than I can count.

Ted Cutcliffe used to be an Army medical helicopter pilot. We call him Tec-9 because of his military background and also because he takes care of problems like a special operations officer. He had been splitting his time between the Birmingham and Charleston restaurants, but when we ran into some operational problems in Charleston, he came in, solved them, and never left. He's my right hand in my new hometown.

Angie Mosier, Angie Mo'! She's a lady who knows how to hang with the boys, whether it's swapping lies, drinking whiskey, or serious cooking. It seems there's not much that Angie can't do in the cooking world. She's a baker who had her own bake shop; she's an incredible photographer; she's a great food stylist, too. We've called on her expertise dozens of times and she's come through with flying colors over and over again.

I met Raquel Pelzel, my editor, in New York. But long before any words had been written, she came by the restaurant, tasted the food, and talked about what the book should look like. Right off the top, I could tell that she was very serious about her work, but not so hard-core that she was unapproachable. I didn't realize then how many cookbooks she'd written. Look her up!

I've never written a book before. Thankfully, I had Sarah Smith at the David Black Agency to shepherd me through this process. She listened to what I wanted from the book, and helped me realize my vision.

I really wanted this book to look and feel fun. Maybe because she's a woman, maybe because she's not a carnivore, but Jerrelle Guy's approach to the photographs was just what the doctor ordered. And she's a joy to hang around! Half the pleasure of working with Jerrelle comes from her partner, Eric Harrison. He did yeoman's work, assisting with both the photographs and the fun. Thanks, my man.

When it came time to write this book, I knew I wanted to work with Lolis Elie. When I met him, he knew what I did and where I was from because he had written about Ricky Scott. Ricky and his family do whole hog barbecue like we do, a few miles up the road in Hell's Half Acre, South Carolina. Lolis and I could talk in a kind of shorthand about where I'm from and what I do. I knew that would make the process a whole lot easier.

—Rodney Scott

I'd be both remiss and manuscript-less were it not for the invaluable assistance of certain people, and I'd like to thank them: my agent, advisor, and friend, David Black; his counsel is wise and generous. Alain Joseph, my personal culinary consultant, read the manuscript with his chef's eyes and improved it significantly. Raquel Pelzel edits like the great writer she is in her other life. And Béatrice and Niriko, whose mutual love of barbecue helped fuel my own enthusiasm.

—Lolis Eric Elie

INDEX

21982319851337